OVERVIEW

Overview

With so much business happening on a global scale, cross-cultural communication is more important than ever before. Communication is always a challenge, and when diverse cultures interact, good communication can be even more challenging. For example, after a major U.S. corporation introduced a new breakfast cereal in Sweden, the company was horrified to discover that the cereal's name translates roughly as "burned peasant" in Swedish.

Imagine the embarrassment, not to mention the loss of revenues that probably ensued. And while this example seems amusing after the fact, cross-cultural miscommunications aren't always benign.

For instance, a large airline manufacturer developed its newest plane model to be flown by two pilots, with both pilots helping and correcting each other.

But what do you suppose happens when the pilots are from a culture in which a subordinate is inhibited by custom from correcting a superior? At least one airline company has had several close calls as a direct result of this "design flaw" – which is ultimately a communication lapse.

Now, you may not be involved in public safety or an industry in which communication errors can cause horrendous mishaps. But you'll likely soon be working with people from different cultures, if you aren't already. You need to learn how to handle cultural differences and maximize your communication opportunities.

And this book will help you do just that. You'll learn about important cultural differences that will help you adapt your communication style to be more effective. In the first topic, you'll learn about the importance of achieving a proper mind-set for cross-cultural communication. In the second topic, you'll study aspects of cultures that affect how people communicate across cultural boundaries. In the third topic, you'll learn about a model of cultural dimensions that will help you enhance your communication abilities.

First topic

In this topic, you'll learn about why cross-cultural communication is so important. You'll also learn why it's beneficial for you to learn how to improve your ability to communicate across cultural boundaries. Then you'll learn about some guidelines for achieving the mind-set that's essential for effective communication.

Second topic

In the second topic, you'll learn about a pioneer who studied and classified important cultural differences. Edward T. Hall was an anthropologist who made early discoveries of factors that differ among cultures. He is known for having identified what he called low-context and high-context factors.

Hall determined that people from low-context cultures communicate explicitly, with words. People from high-context cultures use contextual elements such as shared assumptions, knowledge, and body language to understand each other and communicate.

Third topic

In the third topic, you'll learn about some dimensions common to every culture that affect how people communicate. The cultural model created by Geert Hofstede identifies dimensions of culture – power distance, individualism, masculinity, uncertainty avoidance, and long-term orientation. These dimensions influence how groups, societies, and cultures think about the world and respond to events.

At its conclusion, this topic also presents some important guidelines for communicating effectively based on Hofstede's dimensions.

After you've finished this book, you'll be much more aware of the differences among cultures. And you'll have a good sense of how you need to approach others from different cultures in order to maximize your communication opportunities with them.

But before you begin the book, there is one important disclaimer you should be aware of. The factors and dimensions that Hall and Hofstede identified are often applied to groups and cultures, but not every member of a group behaves the same way. Indeed, groups that operate within societies and cultures often behave differently than the culture itself.

So, if you apply these terms you'll be learning to a culture or group, do it loosely. And know that there will be exceptions within the culture or group.

The globalization of communication has brought with it opportunities to conduct business with people from all over the world. Inevitably, this means interactions and relationships between people who are culturally different. This is known as cross-cultural communication.

A simple definition of a culture is a group of people who share a common set of attitudes, beliefs, and behaviors, and who communicate through common language or symbols.

The culture in which people are socialized influences the manner in which they work, socialize, and interact with others.

If you want to understand and communicate effectively with people of different cultures, it's imperative that you understand how culture affects communication.

Consider the following situations that might happen at a workplace. Do you think these issues signal a problem?

- An employee refuses to make eye contact with the supervisor when they're working together,
- a contract has been signed, yet the customer requests additional negotiation,
- a team leader is habitually late for meetings,
- a customer refuses to answer direct questions about what she requires from a vendor, and
- an employee doesn't contribute to team meetings.

If you answered "yes" or "no" to any of the examples on the previous page, you're probably basing your opinion on the expectations you've developed from your own cultural experiences. But the facts are that each of these business situations may be perfectly acceptable, depending on the culture you work within.

There are many different ways that people of different cultures give and receive information. They communicate in a variety of ways – through talk, silence, expression, emphasis, and gesture. People from different cultures place different emphasis on these methods, and have distinct expectations as to how each should be used to communicate, and what the message is that each conveys.

The best way to understand intercultural communication is to be aware of the five elements of the communication process.

The elements are sender, encoding, channel, decoding, and receiver. To communicate effectively, you'll need to understand the cultural context influencing each of these elements.

Sender

The sender is the person who has something to communicate.

Encoding

Encoding is putting the communication into a form that can be transmitted, such as the written or spoken word.

Channel

The channel is the medium used to transmit the message from sender to receiver.

Decoding

Decoding is receiving and translating the message into meaning.

Receiver

The receiver is the person who accepts and translates the message into meaning.

How a message is sent and received is influenced by the cultural context. A message in any form originating from a sender in one culture and transmitted to a receiver in another culture will be influenced by many variables that will determine the ultimate success of the communication.

In this book, you will learn about the tools you need to make sure effective and appropriate communication takes place when you're in cross-cultural environments.

You'll learn about cultural context, and how this affects the meaning in the messages people send and receive.

You'll also cover speaking and writing in cross-cultural environments, and learn the guidelines for giving presentations for a cross-cultural audience.

Picture the scene. You've been asked to contact some new clients based 3,000 miles away. You've never spoken with them before. You're not sure what approach to take or what response you'll get. But you know it's especially important to be able to communicate effectively in the global community, where cross-cultural issues abound. Thankfully, there are things you can do to improve your cross-cultural communications and ensure that your clients or coworkers across the world become your greatest allies.

It takes time to build working relationships with people from other cultures, but it only takes a second to alienate them by accidentally breaking the rules of intercultural protocols.

That's why relationships are so important in the current global business context, where you have to share the same objectives and the same working space with people with diverse cultural backgrounds.

It's more important than ever to ensure you can understand and appreciate the different cultures you work with. And learning to deal with cultural differences will help you communicate more effectively and create more successful relationships.

In this book, you'll learn how to deal effectively with cultural differences to improve cross-cultural communication.

You'll discover the best practices and strategies that will help you take your cross-cultural communication to a new level.

You'll learn about a structured approach for dealing with cultural differences, and how to adjust your communication style appropriately for different situations.

This book covers the value of becoming aware of your own culture, learning about the other culture, and examining any areas of cultural difference. You'll also learn how to bridge cultural differences by considering four key areas before taking action.

You'll discover how to build rapport across cultures by showing respect and interest, being aware of basic cultural expectations, and getting the other party's name and title right.

In addition, you'll learn about recognizing and overcoming ethnocentrism, stereotyping, and misunderstanding, which are common barriers to effective cross-cultural communication.

CHAPTER 1 - CULTURE AND ITS EFFECT ON COMMUNICATION

CHAPTER 1- Culture and Its Effect on Communication
SECTION I - Understanding Cross-cultural Communication
SECTION II - High-context and Low-context Cross-cultural Communication
SECTION III - Communication and Cultural Dimensions

SECTION I - UNDERSTANDING CROSS-CULTURAL COMMUNICATION

SECTION I - Understanding Cross-cultural Communication

A culture is a collection of beliefs, values, common knowledge, acquired habits, and principles that are shared by a group of people. People from different cultures have their own ways of communicating among themselves. Cultural differences are often responsible for misunderstandings that occur in cross-cultural communications.

To help ease the communication gaps that exist between and among cultures, the discipline of cross-cultural communication provides some useful guidelines. Among the most important is to approach

communication with the proper mind-set. Developing this mind-set requires acknowledging that there are differences among people, being flexible and ready to change when necessary, not imitating or trying to adopt the culture of the people with whom you're interacting, and being aware of barriers and challenges that exist to cross-cultural communication.

Barriers to good communication can be insidious. They include ethnocentrism, or believing in the superiority of one's own ethnic or cultural group; making false assumptions by assigning reasons for someone else's behavior without knowing the person; stereotyping, or generalizing about an individual based on misperceptions made about the person's background or beliefs; and language, which can be a barrier between people who allegedly speak the same one.

ACHIEVING A PROPER MIND-SET

Achieving a proper mind-set

If you were asked to define "culture," what would you say? It's not an easy concept to define because there are many different meanings. For instance, culture can mean the unique ways in which a society or a group expresses itself through the arts, music, and literature. In a larger sense, though, it refers to the shared customary beliefs of ethnic groups and nationalities, as well as subgroups such as organizations.

This course will cover "culture" as it relates to national or ethnic culture. The term encompasses the common knowledge, acquired habits, shared principles, values and beliefs, customs, and unique traditions of ethnic groups, nationalities, and subgroups.

A culture usually contains many diverse elements that all come together to form a coherent whole. It's sometimes easier to understand culture using a metaphor.

For instance, think of a culture as an ecosystem, where there are facets that must coexist and interrelate.

Environment and climate

The environment and climate of an ecosystem support the species of plants and animals that live there. The same applies to a culture. The environment and cultural climate support the people that live within that culture. People are accustomed to the foods grown in their environments, their systems of laws, and their traditions, for example.

Indigenous species

Many diverse plants and animals coexist within an ecosystem. Biodiversity is key to an ecosystem's ability to sustain itself. There may be battles over resources, however. A culture also contains many diverse peoples, elements, and subcultures. Members of a culture aren't uniform – they may not even be similar to each other.

Diversity within a culture is often challenging; people tend to be mistrustful of each other. And, like different species in an ecosystem, different groups within a culture may war over resources.

Cycle of life

Every ecosystem has a cycle of life. Plants and animals both depend on an ecosystem and contribute to its ongoing survival. For instance, plants draw nutrients from the soil, and then enrich the same soil when they die.

A culture is the environment and framework in which children form their values and beliefs as they grow. When grown, people give back to the culture by supporting their institutions, among other things.

Non-indigenous species

Few ecosystems remain completely unchanged over time. Natural shifts in climate or even natural disasters can mean new species are introduced into an established ecosystem. And those species have no choice but to adapt and thrive, or die.

Fundamentals of Cross Cultural Communication

People coming into a new culture must also adapt if they are to survive. They must learn new skills, new habits, new attitudes, and sometimes a new language.

There are many metaphors that can describe a culture. You may have selected one of these. A culture is like a salad, in which all of the ingredients mix together but retain their individual flavors. Or a culture is like an Impressionist painting – there are many different colors and textures, but they all work together to create a coherent whole.

Your culture is the lens through which you see the world. It plays a large role in how you communicate with others. People from different cultures have their own ways of communicating among themselves. Cultural differences are often responsible for the misunderstandings that occur in cross-cultural communications.

To help people learn to communicate better across cultural boundaries, the discipline of cross-cultural communication studies how people from different cultures communicate. This discipline has produced guidelines to help people improve their communication across boundaries.

Question

Now that you know more about cross-cultural communication, why do you think it's important to learn how to communicate effectively across cultural boundaries?

Options:
1. More business is being done globally
2. Most businesses are becoming more diverse

3. Many business owners are interested in being culturally literate

4. Most people want to learn more about other cultures

Answer:

There are many good reasons why you need to learn to communicate across cultural boundaries.

The are several reasons why you need to be able to communicate well across cultural boundaries. First, in a global marketplace, you may find yourself working long-distance or face-to-face with people from different cultures.

Second, businesses are becoming more diverse. You may soon be working on a daily basis with people from different cultures, if you aren't already. Your ability to communicate cross-culturally is crucial to your success.

GUIDELINES FOR ACHIEVING THE MIND-SET

Guidelines for achieving the mind-set
Improving your ability to communicate cross-culturally starts with achieving the right mind-set. There are some guidelines to help you do this, as well as to improve your communications:
- acknowledge there are cultural differences among people,
- be flexible and ready to change,
- don't imitate or try to adopt the culture of the people with whom you're interacting, and
- recognize there are barriers and challenges to overcome.

In order to communicate effectively across cultural boundaries, you must acknowledge that there are differences among people. Don't bury your head in the sand and pretend differences don't exist. It's a myth that people are the same the world over. While humans do share a common nature – everyone eats, sleeps, and laughs – culture plays a key role in shaping how individuals see themselves, think and behave, and interact with the world. People are different.

Question

Consider Tyson. In Tyson's culture, informality and a direct communication style are appreciated. Tyson recently hosted a business meeting with visitors from a culture that values formality. Based on his belief that people are all the same, Tyson assumed that just by being himself, he'd get his message across. Tyson opened his meeting with an amusing story about his family. He then went around the room asking people to identify themselves, and then proceeded to call his visitors by their first names.

Do you think this is an appropriate way for Tyson to have conducted his meeting?

Options:

1. No
2. Yes

Answer:

Tyson should have acknowledged that people in his audience were different from him and used a formal style. He shouldn't have shared personal information, asked people to identify themselves, or used first names.

As a general rule, it's important to acknowledge cultural differences between you and others. Don't assume, as Tyson did, that everyone is the same. If your relationships with people from different cultures do deepen over time, then you'll be able to explore areas of similarity.

Another important guideline for achieving a good mind-set is to be flexible and prepared to change. No matter how earnest and well intentioned you are, assuming others will accept your behavior because you're

Fundamentals of Cross Cultural Communication

"just being you" isn't a good practice. You shouldn't expect others to work around your lack of understanding of their cultural differences.

Instead, you should seek out new techniques and styles for communicating in ways that suit the culture of the people you're dealing with. Don't be afraid to stretch outside your comfort zone to do it.

Consider Luisa's experience. She's worked for 15 years at a company where people don't disagree with each other in public or raise their voices. When Luisa accepts a position in a new company, she finds that her new coworkers engage in arguments and direct disagreement as part of their normal decision-making process.

Initially, Luisa is afraid to disagree or argue with anyone. Eventually, though, she adjusts to her new work environment and learns to present her ideas clearly and without backing down. This helps her integrate into the new company and makes her much more effective at work.

The third guideline for effective cross-cultural communication is don't attempt to imitate or adopt the culture of the people with whom you're interacting. It's easy for others to misinterpret imitation as mockery.

Robert works for an import/export company in a large port city. He's meeting with some new clients from an Asian country. To impress these clients, Robert decides to wear a traditional robe from their culture and conduct a tea ceremony.

Unfortunately, Robert doesn't really understand the importance of the ceremony in his clients' culture, and he doesn't perform it correctly. Rather than being impressed with Robert's efforts, the clients are offended and leave abruptly.

Every culture tends to be protective of its ceremonies and traditions. These events often occupy a special place in a culture, and you can easily offend people by referencing their ceremonies inappropriately.

The last guideline to follow for improving your cross-cultural communication is to recognize the barriers and challenges that exist.

There are many stumbling blocks that prevent people from communicating successfully, and recognizing them is the first step toward overcoming them. Some of the main barriers include ethnocentrism, stereotyping, false assumptions, and language.

Ethnocentrism

Ethnocentrism is a belief in the superiority of your own ethnic or cultural group, and a dislike of all other groups.

For example, the members of the Sales Department tend to applaud themselves for the company's healthy profit picture and downgrade everyone else's contributions. This ethnocentrist view causes others in the company to avoid working with the Sales Department, and its members are becoming isolated.

Stereotyping

Stereotyping is when you have a mental construct about a group that's strongly positive or strongly negative. Based on this image, you categorize people and generalize about them. Stereotyping can be very dangerous. It can prevent people from listening to each other and building good relationships. For instance, believing that all red-headed people have hot tempers is a stereotype.

False assumptions

False assumptions can result when you assign causes to someone else's behavior without knowing them. Assumptions can reveal you have a bias for or against another person.

For example, if you think that someone is rude for not saying please or thank you, you may be making a false assumption. The person's behavior may simply be a cultural norm.

Language

Language is one of the most frustrating barriers, and can be challenging even among people who supposedly speak the same language.

As an example, Anna is working on two projects simultaneously, but one is winding down. When Anna's boss asks her whether she has time to take on another assignment, Anna says "yes." To Anna, "yes" means she has a little bit of time available. To her boss, "yes" means Anna can devote herself 100% to a new project, starting now. Even though Anna and her boss share a cultural background, they miscommunicate and cause a problem.

Another tricky point about language is that, in some cultures, people don't ask questions. Questions are considered a sign of ignorance or lack of intelligence. So, even if you ask people from these cultures whether they understand what you've told them, you usually get a reaffirming, positive answer. In dealing with these situations, it's important to present information in different ways, using different media. For instance, a presentation should be accompanied by handouts with words and diagrams, if appropriate.

To avoid misunderstandings and make sure that everyone understands what's being said, it's important that you follow some simple communication guidelines:
- use plain, simple language,
- avoid slang, jargon, idioms, and colloquialisms,
- use short, simple sentences,
- speak slowly, but not overly loudly,
- enunciate clearly, and
- clarify whether people understand by asking questions.

Question

What are the guidelines for successful cross-cultural communication?

Options:

1. Engage with a different culture but don't imitate it
2. Recognize barriers and challenges to cross-cultural communication
3. Acknowledge that people are the same the world over
4. Adopt other people's cultures
5. Acknowledge the differences among people from different cultures
6. Be flexible and prepared to change

Answer:

Option 1: This option is correct. Imitation can cause offense. It's best to be polite and curious about others, but don't try to adopt the culture you're interacting with.

Option 2: This option is correct. There are many stumbling blocks that hinder people from communicating across cultures. These include ethnocentrism, stereotyping, false assumptions, and language.

Recognizing barriers and challenges to cross-cultural communication is the first step to overcoming them.

Option 3: This option is not correct. This is a myth. Humans share many characteristics, but people are different.

Option 4: This option is not correct. Attempting to adopt elements from another person's culture may look like flattery, or it could look as though you're making fun of that culture. Avoid this.

Option 5: This option is correct. People's beliefs, values, customs, traditions, and languages are sometimes very different. In learning to communicate cross-culturally, you need to acknowledge this.

Option 6: This option is correct. You won't get anywhere unless you're able to extend yourself to learn new communication styles.

SECTION II - HIGH-CONTEXT AND LOW-CONTEXT CROSS-CULTURAL COMMUNICATION

SECTION II - High-context and Low-context Cross-cultural Communication

People of different cultures, societies, and groups often communicate very differently from each other. This can make the task of communicating across cultural boundaries a very tricky one.

The anthropologist Edward T. Hall studied differences in communication styles among cultures and groups. He developed the terms "low-context" and "high-context" to describe basic differences. No culture or group is entirely low- or high-context. Within any group there's a range of behaviors.

Low-context cultures include the US, Canada, Germany, and Scandinavia. People in these cultures generally use direct, explicit, verbal communication. People rely on facts and verbal explanations, not intuition, nonverbal cues, or common assumptions.

People in high-context cultures – China, Korea, Japan, and the Arab countries, for example – tend to use indirect, circular communication. People share common assumptions, beliefs, and knowledge that enable them to communicate without relying only on words.

LOW-CONTEXT AND HIGH-CONTEXT CULTURES

Low-context and high-context cultures

Roberta, a Canadian executive, is in Japan to negotiate a contract with executives at an automobile supply company. During the talks, Roberta makes explicit, direct statements and demands. She notices the Japanese executives becoming more and more uncomfortable as she speaks, but she ignores their reactions. Before too long, one of the executives politely calls an end to the meeting, and the Japanese executives walk out.

Roberta is dumbfounded. What do you suppose happened? Well, it turns out the Japanese executives were deeply offended by her communication style.

Roberta comes from a low-context culture, where communication happens primarily with words, either oral or written. In low-context cultures, it's expected that discussions will be direct, and that each side will express demands clearly and explicitly.

The Japanese executives, on the other hand, come from a high-context culture. In this kind of culture, much of the meaning people get from communication comes from subtle, nonverbal cues, shared assumptions, and knowledge gleaned from long-term relationships. Communicating directly may be considered offensive, and making demands can be interpreted as a sign of ignorance.

The terms "low-context" and "high-context" were developed by anthropologist Edward T. Hall. They're useful, broad-based descriptions of differences in communication styles between societies, ethnic groups, and cultures. Being aware of these differences can help you learn to communicate across cultural boundaries.

Low-context

In a low-context culture, people rely primarily on words for communication. In general, they don't pay much attention to body language, social status, or their intuition. People in low-context cultures have many connections with others, but many of their relationships are of short duration.

High-context

In a high-context culture, people have close, long-term connections with each other. People know what to do and what to think from being raised with the same social norms, beliefs, and expectations. High-context cultures rely less on words and more on intuition, facial expressions, tone of voice, gestures, and the social status of the individuals.

Low- and high-context behaviors are evident in groups within a culture as well as in societies and cultures as a whole.

For example, many community action groups are low-context. Members are acquainted with each other, but relationships usually aren't deep or lasting. Verbal instructions are key to organizing and directing people in what to do.

Your family is likely an example of a high-context group. You're steeped in your family's values and beliefs, and you know your role. You know how to behave within the family unit and what's expected of you, and you act accordingly.

Throughout the world, there's a range of low-context to high-context cultures, societies, and groups. As you move along the range from low-context to high-context, communication becomes less explicit and more intuitive. Cultures that are considered lowest-context include the German and Scandinavian cultures. The highest-context cultures include Korea, China, and Japan.

But remember that as useful as the low-context and high-context labels are in describing overall communication within a culture, they can be misleading. No culture is completely low- or high-context.

For instance, groups and individuals within a predominantly low-context culture sometimes operate in a high-context manner, and vice versa. People who've worked together for a long time may know each other very well and act in a high-context manner. They may communicate as much through context as they do through words.

Because of the many variations within a culture, it's important not to apply the terms low- and high- context to entire cultures – especially when a culture may include people of many different nationalities and ethnicities. It's more accurate to apply the terms to situations and events.

Question

Match the communication styles with the statements that describe them. Each communication style may have more than one match.

Options:

A. High-context
B. Low-context

Targets:

1. People have close, long-term connections
2. People have many connections with others, but relationships are of short duration
3. Most people know how to behave and think from years of interaction with each other
4. People rely mostly on words for communication
5. Communication depends on nonverbal cues

Answer:

In a high-context group, people maintain close relationships over a long period of time.

In a low-context group, people tend to have many acquaintances but only a few long-term relationships. People in high-context groups know the group's unwritten rules of behavior and thought.

Low-context groups depend on words to instruct each other and outsiders how to behave and think. High-context groups rely on body language, social cues, and status within the group for meaning.

LOW-CONTEXT COMMUNICATION

Low-context communication

With the basic definitions behind you, you're ready to learn more about low- and high-context communication, beginning with low-context. Nadia is a financial analyst based in New York. Today, she's meeting with a colleague, Chang, to discuss a new business initiative.

Follow along as Nadia and Chang discuss Chang's idea. Think about how the two coworkers relate to each other.

Nadia: I don't think your idea is workable, Chang. I mean, it's not going to provide that many benefits, and it'll be costly to implement.

Nadia is doubtful and negative.

Chang: I disagree with you. I say the benefits are worth the costs.

Chang is argumentative.

Nadia: Well, then, let's line up the facts and evaluate them, one after another. My intuition tells me it won't work, but I'll change my mind if the facts tell me otherwise.

Nadia is argumentative.

Chang: Good. The facts will show specifically why my idea is the best one for saving the company money.

Chang is determined.

Question

You'll learn more about low-context communication characteristics shortly. But based on the previous scenario, what do you think are the characteristics of low-context communication?

Options:

1. It's direct and to the point
2. It's logical and sequenced
3. Information is spelled out
4. Meaning is contained in the message
5. Emotions are as important as words
6. Feelings align with meaning

Answer:

On the pages that follow, you'll learn more about how Nadia and Chang's discussion contained elements of low-context communication.

Low-context communication has distinct characteristics that distinguish it from high-context communication.

It's direct and to the point

Since meaning is conveyed primarily using words alone, people are direct and to the point. They try to be precise and avoid extra verbiage, which helps to avoid miscommunication. Both Nadia and Chang spoke very plainly; they didn't embellish.

It's logical and sequenced

Low-context communication is also logical. There's a strong belief that there's always an objective truth that can be reached through linear processes of discovery. As Nadia stated, "Let's line up the facts and evaluate them."

Information is spelled out

Information is spelled out in detail, leaving nothing open to interpretation and misunderstanding. As Chang said, "The facts will show specifically why my idea is the best one for saving the company money."

Meaning is contained in the message

Low-context communication relies on words, not on context, to convey meaning.

Feelings align with meaning

People don't say "yes" when they mean "no" or "maybe." As in the example, both Nadia and Chang felt free to express their emotions as they disagreed with each other.

Because of the apparent openness and abundance of written and oral information that's available, low-context societies and groups are relatively easy for an outsider to join. However, looks can be deceiving.

While you'll likely be welcomed into such a group or society, you'll probably find that it has a high-context core group that makes the decisions and has the power. It will take time to build the knowledge and relationships required to become part of this core group.

HIGH-CONTEXT COMMUNICATION

High-context communication
You've learned about low-context communication. Now, turn your attention to the other end of the spectrum – high-context communication.

In high-context communication, words alone aren't used to explain or instruct. Instead, words evoke past experiences and knowledge, which people use to deduce meaning. People hear one word and understand ten.

Consider this example. A prominent advertising executive galvanizes his team into action with the phrase, "There is a tide..." The phrase, from a Shakespeare play, refers to seizing an opportunity before the opposition has time to gather strength. When they hear the phrase, team members put their current workloads aside and pool their resources – they know they're being called to action.

The reason the team members know how to respond is that they share common experiences and knowledge about the business and past activity. They think, "This has happened before; it's happening again," and they know their roles and what to do.

Think of high-context communication as the tip of an iceberg – most of the meaning lies below the surface and is never verbalized. In fact, verbal explanations may be considered insulting in high-context groups. They imply that listeners aren't socialized or knowledgeable enough to understand what's being said. In the previous example, team members were expected to know what their leader meant at the unexpressed level – below the water line – when he uttered that phrase.

If you're a low-context communicator, it can be difficult to learn to communicate within a high-context group. However, knowing some common characteristics of high-context communication can help you avoid missteps. High-context communication is indirect. It happens in a cyclical rather than logical order. It's also understated, and attention is given to nonverbal behavior and cues.

Indirect

High-context communication pays more attention to relationships and people than it does to information. Speakers are indirect, being careful not to cause embarrassment, hurt feelings, or offense. In many cases, they're formal and polite.

For example, rather than say, "Your work isn't very good," a high-context communicator might say, "I'd like you to give this issue some more thought" or ask, "Have you been under some stress in the last week?"

Cyclical order

High-context communication doesn't move in a logical order from point A to point B to point C. It jumps back and forth and omits details, assuming these details are understood by everyone. A discussion often cycles back repeatedly to topics already discussed.

For example, Pierre creates an agenda that's simply a list of items to be covered. During his meeting, Pierre encourages team members to address items as they wish. He lets discussions flow naturally and allows people to go back and discuss items the group already addressed.

Understated

High-context communication tends to be understated – reserved, restrained, and impersonal.

For instance, in presenting his qualifications for a new job, Raoul is modest about his achievements. He doesn't flaunt his experience or his excellent work with teams, since he doesn't want to take credit for work performed by others.

Attention to nonverbal behaviors and cues

Nonverbal behaviors such as gestures, body language, silence, and physical proximity are used extensively to convey meaning.

For instance, through long experience, the members of Ram's project team know how to read his moods, facial expressions, and silences. By watching Ram, members know when to speak, how much explanation to give, and when to be silent.

Because so much meaning lies beneath the surface in high-context communication, it can be very difficult for a low-context communicator to join or participate in a culture that uses this form of communication. It generally takes a long time to build up the relationships and knowledge required to effectively give and receive meaning.

Question

Now that you know more about high- and low-context characteristics, classify examples of communication styles as being high- or low-context.

Options:

A. At the family reunion, the eldest woman presents everyone with a photograph of her parents, with their names written on the back

B. When Ed balks at Tom's demands, Tom redoubles his efforts to argue Ed into agreeing to what he wants

C. Maya asks Juan what he liked about her presentation; Juan replies, "Many of the listeners seemed pleased with what you said"

D. Sean and Ahmed meet to discuss a contract; Sean says, "Let's get everything out on the table"

Targets:

1. Low-context
2. High-context

Answer:

Low-context communication is verbal. People express themselves with words and aren't afraid to speak their minds.

High-context communication is nonverbal and nuanced. A photograph can remind people of where they come from. A person will resist criticizing a coworker.

SECTION III - COMMUNICATION AND CULTURAL DIMENSIONS

SECTION III - Communication and Cultural Dimensions

Geert Hofstede's Model of Cultural Dimensions identifies four dimensions that define the differences among cultures: power distance, individualism, masculinity, and uncertainty avoidance.

Power distance assesses the degree to which the less powerful members of a culture, institution, or organization accept the unequal distribution of power. People from cultures with a high power distance tend to accept inequality. In a culture with a low power distance, people tend to believe they're all created equal.

Individualism and its opposite, collectivism, assess the degree to which people are integrated into groups. In a highly individualistic culture, ties between people are loose and individual rights are important. In a collectivist culture, people are born into social groups in which they may live their entire lives.

Masculinity, along with femininity, refers to the distribution of roles between the genders. In a masculine culture, gender roles are fixed, with men being dominant. Men are assertive and women are nurturing. In a more feminine culture, the roles between the two genders are more fluid, with both men and women sharing assertive and nurturing roles.

Uncertainty avoidance assesses a culture's tolerance for uncertainty, ambiguity, and risk. A culture with a strong uncertainty avoidance is risk averse, preferring tried and true, traditional methods. A culture with weak uncertainty avoidance is more accepting of ambiguity.

HOFSTEDE'S MODEL OF CULTURAL DIMENSIONS

Hofstede's Model of Cultural Dimensions

Suppose that traveling to distant lands has always been a dream of yours. Then one day, you're presented with an opportunity to take a work assignment in a foreign country. You know it's the opportunity of a lifetime, but you're nervous. How will you fit in? How will you learn to interact with people, to understand and not insult them unintentionally? What you need is a model for learning about and interacting with the new culture you'll be entering.

There are many models and theories for describing, summarizing, and analyzing national cultures. One of the most quoted and widely discussed is Geert Hofstede's Model of Cultural Dimensions.

In 1980, Geert Hofstede, a social scientist from the Netherlands, studied the impact of culture on behavior by examining the values and beliefs of 116,000 IBM employees. It was one of the most comprehensive studies of culture, spanning 64 different countries.

The result of Hofstede's study was the identification of four national, cultural dimensions: power distance, individualism, masculinity, and uncertainty avoidance. A fifth dimension – long-term orientation – was added later to distinguish among cultures on the basis of how people think about the past, present, and future. This last dimension won't be covered in this course.

Hofstede went further than simply identifying the dimensions – he scored different areas of the world on how thoroughly they incorporate each dimension. Hofstede's ratings are based on a scale from 1 to 120.

Using Hofstede's ratings, you can compare different countries and say, for example, that Australia is more individualistic than Ecuador.

Be careful with these ratings, though – every culture has many subcultures that can differ substantially from each other. And globalization and the Internet are changing people's behaviors all across the world. Hofstede's scores are averages calculated from survey scores. To apply a single score to an entire culture could be misleading.

POWER DISTANCE AND INDIVIDUALISM

Power distance and individualism

The first dimension in Hofstede's model is called power distance. Power distance measures the degree to which the less powerful members of a culture, institution, or organization accept the unequal distribution of power.

The power distance concept is easily observed within a family. Children naturally accept that their parents have more power than they do. They expect their parents, as adults and caretakers, to have special privileges. Some parents are authoritarian and maintain a high power distance from their children. Others want their children to regard them more as friends. They maintain a low power distance from their children.

The same extremes of power distance relationships exist in cultures.

High power distance

People from cultures with a high power distance tend to accept inequality. In these cultures, there's often a rigid social structure, with bosses being authoritarian and psychologically distant from workers. Workers don't expect to be asked for their opinions or participate in decision-making. They tend to wait for instructions from above.

Low power distance

People from cultures with a low power distance tend to have the perspective that "everyone is created equal." They're used to people in power being available, and to trusting them. Bosses often ask their workers for their thoughts and opinions, and listen to them.

Differences in power distance can cause communication problems. Follow along as Shane talks to his coworker, Phoebe, about a recent conversation he had with his new boss.

Shane: I think I'm in trouble, Phoebe. I went to see my new boss, Ryan, about my first assignment. He started to get really detailed about what he wanted me to do. I thought I'd save him some time and told him I didn't need his direction. He got very quiet, but he seemed upset with me.

Phoebe: Ryan always gives very detailed instructions. You'll need to listen to him. He's a very formal guy, too, and he doesn't socialize with other managers or with us.

Shane: Uh oh. I guess I shouldn't have slapped him on the back then!

Question

What do you think happened between Shane and Ryan?

Options:

1. Shane created a problem by acting inappropriately in a low power distance manner

2. Shane tried to save Ryan some time, when he should have listened to Ryan's instructions

3. Ryan didn't react properly to Shane's offer; he should have stopped giving instructions

4. Shane should have adopted a low power distance manner when talking with Ryan

Answer

Option 1: This option is correct. The differences in the power distance preferences of the two men caused a problem. Shane was informal and casual, and Ryan was offended.

Option 2: This option is correct. As a high power distance person, Ryan gives detailed instructions with his assignments. Shane should have listened.

Option 3: This option is not correct. Ryan is the boss. Shane can't change Ryan; he can only change his own reactions to other people.

Option 4: This option is not correct. Adopting a low power distance manner is exactly what Shane did, to his eventual dismay.

A second Hofstede dimension is individualism. Individualism and its opposite, collectivism, measure the degree to which people are integrated into groups.

In an individualistic culture, ties between individuals are loose. Personal achievement and individual rights are important. Teamwork is important too, but individual contributions are expected and rewarded. People communicate primarily through words and largely ignore nonverbal communication. Their communication focuses mostly on conveying information.

At the other end of the spectrum is collectivism. In a collectivist culture, people are born into strong and cohesive social groups. They remain in these groups, often their extended families, throughout their lives. The group is more important than the individual. Conformity is expected and rewarded. Communication relies on shared knowledge and assumptions, as well as intuition, social status, and other nonverbal cues. Communication focuses primarily on building and maintaining relationships.

Question

Now that you've learned about power distance and individualism, match each dimension with the appropriate description.

Options:

A. Individualism

B. Collectivism

C. High power distance

D. Low power distance

Targets:

1. People have loose ties to each other, with a few close relationships; communication is primarily word-based and used to convey information

2. People are born into their social groups, which are like extended families; communication is based on shared knowledge and assumptions, and used to maintain relationships

3. People believe that power is distributed unequally and that those in power should be entitled to special privileges

4. People don't tolerate inequality; they believe in equality and that those in power can be trusted

Answer:

People in individualistic cultures have many acquaintances but few close relationships.

Communication relies on words and is used to convey information.

In collectivist cultures, people are born into their social groups, in which they often live their entire lives. Relationships are very important, and communication is used primarily to maintain relationships.

In a culture with high power distance, people accept inequality. They expect their leaders to enjoy privileges and to exhibit the trappings of power.

In a culture with low power distance, people don't tolerate being unequal. They tend to trust the people in power.

MASCULINITY AND UNCERTAINTY AVOIDANCE

Masculinity and uncertainty avoidance
Another dimension in Hofstede's model is masculinity. Paired with femininity, this dimension refers to the distribution of roles between the genders.
Question
Before moving on to learn about masculine and feminine cultures, how would you characterize a masculine culture?
Options:
1. Gender roles are clearly defined
2. Men are dominant and women are nurturing
3. Money and possessions are important
4. Gender roles are fluid
5. Conflicts are resolved through negotiation
6. Aggression is acceptable and often used to resolve conflicts
Answer:
You didn't select the appropriate characteristics. Now, you'll learn more about a masculine culture.

As you may have correctly identified, in masculine cultures, men are assertive and women are nurturing. Gender roles are clearly defined. Men dominate society. It's acceptable to resolve conflicts through aggression. Performance matters, and achievers are admired. Independence is ideal, and money and possessions are important.

At the other end of the spectrum is the feminine culture. In a feminine culture, men assume nurturing as well as assertive roles. Gender roles are fluid and there is more equality between the sexes. Quality of life, people, and the environment are valued. Interdependence is the ideal.

The fourth dimension in Hofstede's model, and the last one covered in this course, is called uncertainty avoidance. This dimension assesses a culture's tolerance for uncertainty, risk, ambiguity, and unstructured situations. An unstructured situation is an event that's new and different from the "usual."

Question

Before learning more about uncertainty avoidance, think about this: how comfortable are you with risk and ambiguity?

Options:

1. I avoid risk and uncertainty at all costs
2. I'm OK with a low level of risk and ambiguity
3. Uncertainty doesn't bother me – I'm a risk-taker

Answer:

Option 1: You have strong uncertainty avoidance. Many people feel as you do.

Option 2: You're in good company – many people feel as you do. You tend toward strong uncertainty avoidance.

Option 3: You have weak uncertainty avoidance. This suggests that risk-taking behavior is natural for you.

People in strong uncertainty avoidance cultures consider uncertainty a threat they must fight. They reject change and prefer to use tried and true, traditional methods.

People often have a fatalistic world view. They may have high stress levels because they don't feel fully in control. And they're often less willing to make decisions that involve elements of the unknown.

Disagreements between people occur frequently and are highly vocal. There's a general intolerance for multiple points of view, and people work toward eliminating alternative opinions. In general, people with a strong uncertainty avoidance prefer highly structured situations, strict rules, and law and order.

In cultures with weak uncertainty avoidance, on the other hand, life is lived "as it comes." There's less stress and anxiety. People are willing to take risks, and there's more openness to ambiguity.

Dissent is accepted and people are encouraged to take risks. There are as few rules as possible, and the emphasis is on common sense.

Question

Having learned about the cultural dimensions masculinity and uncertainty avoidance, match each dimension with its description.

Options:
A. Masculinity
B. Femininity
C. Strong uncertainty avoidance
D. Weak uncertainty avoidance

Targets:
1. Men dominate the culture and women occupy traditional female roles; work is important because it provides status and material goods
2. Gender roles aren't fixed; quality of life is as important as work
3. People strongly prefer structured situations; tradition is important; change isn't welcomed
4. People tolerate risk; they're more comfortable with new, unstructured situations; entrepreneurship may flourish

Answer:

Masculinity defines cultures in which men are the dominant gender. Masculine cultures value work and personal achievement, and often prefer aggression to negotiation.

Femininity defines cultures in which gender roles aren't fixed. Feminine cultures value quality of life and prefer negotiation to aggression.

A culture with strong uncertainty avoidance emphasizes tradition and "the way things have always been done." Risk is to be avoided, and change isn't welcome.

A culture with weak uncertainty avoidance shows a tolerance for risk and unstructured situations. Risk-taking and entrepreneurship are rewarded.

x

USING HOFSTEDE'S MODEL FOR COMMUNICATION

Using Hofstede's model for communication

The advantage of using a model like Hofstede's is that it enables you to learn about cultures through a finite number of dimensions.

If you're familiar with Hofstede's dimensions and you can determine which dimensions are being exhibited by the people you're working with, there are guidelines you can use for communicating with them.

Power distance

If you're dealing with people from a higher power distance culture than yours, remember that they prefer strong guidance. They're not used to being asked for their opinions or participating in decision- making.

To communicate effectively with them, you must provide clear and explicit directions. You should also work on getting people to trust you. Show them their opinions and ideas are important to you, and invite them into your decision-making process.

At the other end of the spectrum, you may be dealing with people with a lower power distance than yours. When this is the case, be prepared to operate in an informal environment. People may address you by your first name and may not accord you the deference you're used to. They may also want to get to know you on a personal level.

When communicating with someone from a low power distance culture, you may need to pull back so that you're not too commanding and domineering. People don't need as much leadership and guidance, and may even resent it.

Also, remember that people in low power distance cultures expect their bosses to be accessible to them and open to their opinions. If you're in a position of power, you should make yourself available and open up the lines of communication.

Individualism

If you're working with people who have higher individualism than you do, be prepared for an environment that relies less on relationships and more on the spoken and written word. People are goal-oriented and strive for personal achievement.

When communicating with individualists, you may need to foster greater team collaboration and team spirit. Individualists will want to keep ideas and information to themselves, but should be encouraged to share.

At the other end of the spectrum, if you're dealing with people from a collectivist culture, bear in mind that people's family lives may take precedence over their work lives.

People are used to working in groups, so they may not be used to taking personal responsibility. Encourage them to take responsibility for themselves and their actions.

Masculinity

If you're working with people from a culture that is more masculine than yours, understand that people will be very focused on work. They'll expect long working hours and discuss business everywhere, even in social situations. Personal questions are regarded as intrusive. The best communication style in this environment is direct, concise, and unemotional.

In addition, be prepared to encourage balance if there is aggression. Focus on quality of life, and "working to live" instead of "living to work" ethics. Talking about achievement, promotion, and success will motivate people in a masculine culture.

In a more feminine culture, on the other hand, you need to understand that people value their personal time. Personal questions are normal, and help establish relationships. Trust is more important than achievement and accomplishments, and is earned over time.

Appeal to people's sensitive sides by reinforcing what they believe in – quality of life. Don't talk about material things or be too aggressive, particularly if you're selling, as they will find this disconcerting.

Uncertainty avoidance

If you're working with people who have a strong uncertainty avoidance, be prepared for resistance to any new ideas that may lead to risk or increased uncertainty.

Be careful to back up your proposals with facts; people may automatically oppose threatening new ideas. Give people time to understand new ideas in their own ways.

If you're working in a culture with a weak uncertainty avoidance, try to be more open to new ideas. Give people guidance, but then let them execute their ideas independently.

When communicating with low uncertainty avoidance cultures, you may want to control the risk-taking as much as you can.

Knowing the guidelines for communicating with people of different cultural backgrounds is invaluable to the improvement of your own cross-cultural communication.

Question 1 of 2

Match the dimensions with the appropriate guidelines.

Options:

A. High power distance
B. Low power distance
C. Individualism
D. Collectivism

Targets:

1. People expect strong leadership and guidance; show people their opinions matter to you

2. Provide autonomy, share personal information, and ask people to participate in decision-making

\3. Persuade people to share information; try to build team spirit and enthusiasm for working in teams

4. Encourage people to take greater personal responsibility for their actions

Answer:

People from high power distance cultures aren't used to being asked for ideas. You must build trust and show them that they and their opinions are important to you. Also, if you're in a position of power, be sure to provide a strong level of guidance and leadership.

People from a lower power distance culture are used to a casual style and a certain amount of independence. They may want to establish relationships with you. In any case, give them autonomy to do work their own way, and ask them to help in decision-making.

Individualists prefer to keep information to themselves and work independently. They should be encouraged to collaborate and work in teams.

People in collectivist cultures may hide behind the group; they need to be encouraged to take responsibility for themselves.

Question 2 of 2

Match each dimension with the appropriate guidelines.

Options:

A. Masculinity

B. Femininity

C. Weak uncertainty avoidance

D. Strong uncertainty avoidance

Targets:

1. Use a direct, concise, and unemotional style

2. Avoid discussion of material things, and focus on quality of life issues

3. Control risk-taking behaviors; give people guidance, but let them execute ideas on their own

4. Give people time to get used to new ideas; back up proposals with facts to prevent people from being able to negate your ideas

Answer:

A masculine culture emphasizes performance, achievement, and the value of work. To communicate effectively, you need to be concise and direct.

A feminine culture is a "work to live" culture that values quality of life. Focusing on achievement, performance, and materialism may be distressing to people in a feminine culture.

People with weak uncertainty avoidance are comfortable with risk and ambiguity. You should provide guidance as necessary, but don't over-manage. Let people execute ideas as they see fit.

A culture with a high uncertainty avoidance will automatically fight new ideas that conflict with traditional ways and methods. So back up your proposals with facts, and give people time to get used to new ideas.

CHAPTER 2 - COMMUNICATING ACROSS CULTURES

CHAPTER 2 - Communicating Across Cultures
SECTION I - Speaking and Writing Across Cultures
SECTION II - Effective Cross-cultural Presentations

SECTION I - SPEAKING AND WRITING ACROSS CULTURES

SECTION I - Speaking and Writing Across Cultures

Culture consists of the values, attitudes, and behaviors in a given group. In cross-cultural communication, it's important to understand the role of context. In low-context cultures, communication is explicit, meaning messages are conveyed through the literal meaning of the words. In high-context communication, meaning is inferred from the message context, rather than from its content.

CULTURAL COMMUNICATION

Cultural communication
The reality of global interconnectedness means that modern businesspeople need a greater awareness of diversity than ever before. Despite the proliferation of devices that enable instant contact almost anywhere in the world, real communication depends on understanding the differences in people's cultural orientation and patterns of thinking.

People don't choose what country to be born into, which immediate advantages their status will bring, or which language they'll first speak.

But, as they grow from infants to adults, they learn how to understand and interpret communication based on the societal rules that go along with these conditions. This varies greatly from culture to culture.

When you're communicating across cultural boundaries, your success will be affected by how you present your message, and how that message will be interpreted within a particular social context.

Fundamentals of Cross Cultural Communication

Many businesspeople operate on the assumption that their own ways of communicating will be understood and accepted by other people.

They fail to recognize that interpersonal work or social relationships can go wrong simply because someone in the relationship misreads verbal, nonverbal, or written communication signals.

When you can understand and can communicate effectively in a cross-cultural environment, you'll avoid these misunderstandings and cultural faux-pas.

Cultural communication is a culture's system for creating, sending, and processing the information that guides people's assumptions and behaviors. To avoid going off track in cross-cultural situations, you'll need to be aware of how to communicate in the context of other parties' cultural preferences, expectations, and style.

HIGH-CONTEXT AND LOW-CONTEXT CULTURES

High-context and low-context cultures
One of the distinguishing characteristics of a culture is context orientation. Context is the environment surrounding a communication. Put simply, how much the environment surrounding a communication changes or informs its meaning. Cultures range from low-context to high-context.

High-context
In high-context cultures, much of the communication is implicit. People understand the implied meanings arising from physical settings, relationships, or shared understandings. When people communicate, the unspoken is as rich in meaning as the spoken or written word.

Low-context
In low-context cultures, most communication is explicit. People gain understanding from the literal meaning of written and spoken words, regardless of the context.

Fundamentals of Cross Cultural Communication

When people communicate, messages are presented and received in a logical, linear sequence.

World cultures can be placed along a sliding scale from high- to low-context. Whenever you're communicating with someone, you should try to understand where that person falls along this scale, and tailor your communication style accordingly.

Although no culture exists entirely at one or the other end of the scale, Japan, China, and Korea are examples of high-context cultures. Canada, the United States, Germany, and the Scandinavian countries are considered to be low-context cultures.

Whenever you're communicating with someone, it's important to consider where that person falls along the contextual scale, and to tailor your communication style accordingly. Cross-cultural communicators who don't understand each other's context often come to different conclusions about what messages have been sent and received.

Phillip is a low-context communicator who is on a business trip to a high-context culture. It's now Friday and he's leaving Saturday evening, but wants to meet with Dao before he goes. Follow along as Phillip tries to arrange the business meeting with Dao.

Phillip: Dao, I'm glad I ran into you. I'm leaving Saturday night and I want to meet with you that afternoon.

Dao: There's supposed to be lovely weather tomorrow.

Phillip: Uh-huh. So can you be here by noon?

Dao: Yes. Saturday is traditionally a day we spend with family.

Phillip: Yeah. I'm looking forward to going home. So, I'll book a room for the meeting.

Dao: Saturday is my eldest son's birthday.

Phillip: Oh, well, tell him happy birthday from me.
Dao: Thank you, I will.

Question

So what do you think happened at the business meeting on Saturday?

Options:

1. Phillip showed up for the meeting, but Dao didn't
2. Dao showed up for the meeting but Phillip didn't
3. Both Phillip and Dao showed up for the meeting

Answer:

Option 1: This is the correct option. Phillip didn't understand the implicit meaning of the message Dao was sending him. Although she said yes to the meeting, she assumed that Phillip would understand that it was a polite way of not contradicting him.

Option 2: This option is incorrect. Dao was a high-context communicator. When she mentioned the weather on Saturday, that the day was traditionally spent with family, and that it was her son's birthday she was indicating she couldn't make the meeting.

Option 3: This option is incorrect. The implicit meaning in Dao's response to the meeting request was that she was busy on Saturday. Although it wasn't his intention, Phillip's request to pass on birthday greetings to Dao's son would have been interpreted by her to mean Phillip understood that she had other plans.

Describing a culture as high- or low-context is a form of sociotyping – a means of accurately describing members of a group by their general traits. This is useful as a basis for understanding how people communicate.

Communication in high-context cultures

In high-context cultures, people derive significant meaning from implicit communication. This means a communicated message is strongly influenced by unspoken, but understood, influences.

There are a number of techniques that will be of benefit in high-context communication:
- adapt your communication style to the style and status of the other person,
- remember to use formal titles,
- avoid being too direct or contradictory,
- be respectful of the silence and conversation gaps,
- use social and relational conversation to establish your relationship, and
- use silence to carefully consider points and decisions before you verbalize them.

For example, in a high-context culture, establishing relationships is an essential part of business. There are often extensive introductions and social interactions before business takes place. During these interactions, communicators devote considerable time to social and relational conversations. This is an indirect way of determining a person's status, knowledge, and potential for a relationship.

You should avoid direct communication or contradiction, especially during these early stages of a relationship. In a high-context culture, significant meaning is imbued in symbols, protocol, and formal forms of address, especially when there is a difference in status between the participants.

For example, gifts are sometimes offered as a sign of respect, a token of appreciation, or an indication that a business association is progressing well. The age, social status, and rank of an individual in relation to your own will dictate the style of communication that you should use in high-context communication.

To respect someone's status, it's important to adapt your style to the person with whom you're communicating. The level of respect you should show depends on the disparity between your status and the receiver. In any high-context situation, it's important to be polite and reserved. When you speak or write to people, you should acknowledge their status by using their formal or business title, such as Doctor, General Manager, or Professor.

In low-context cultures, gaps in the conversation make people uncomfortable. But in high-context cultures, silence is respected. It's important for people to show that they're taking the time to process information and think about a response. They may also use silence as a way to disagree implicitly. This is because a direct negative answer is considered impolite. During the silence, a negative response may be conveyed through body language, such as folding the hands or frowning slightly.

When you're communicating in a high-context culture, you shouldn't feel obliged to fill silences – silence is generally seen as acceptable as an occasion for reflection. In high-context cultures, effective written communication reflects the relationship between the sender and receiver, and is imbued with the appropriate level of formality. It's important to provide background information about you, so the receiver can put the message in context.

High-context correspondence should emphasize respect for the status of the receiver. As with conversation, you should avoid being too direct, as this may be considered rude.

There are some common characteristics of high-context communication:
- it's characterized by diplomacy, implicit messages, and group harmony,
- there is high use of indirect message elements such as vocal tone, and body language,
- there is an emphasis on developing long-term relationships,
- conflict is discouraged, and must be resolved before work can progress, and
- communication is personalized.

Communication in low-context cultures

In low-context cultures, people communicate directly and explicitly and rely mainly on verbal communication. In general, casual and friendly speech patterns and the use of slang are more acceptable than in high-context cultures.

There are a number of techniques that will be of benefit in low-context communication:
- be factual and direct,
- speak up if you have an opposing viewpoint,
- use casual and friendly speech patterns,
- keep social conversation to a minimum, and
- use silence to indicate you have nothing left to say or that it's time to move to a different subject.

Communication is usually linear, moving quickly from one subject to the next. This is particularly true in business, where time is equated with money. In both verbal and written low-context communication, others will expect you to be frank about your opinions, and to contradict ideas and information with which you don't agree.

In high-context cultures, silence is acceptable and used as time for thought. In low-context cultures, silence is seen as awkward – a sign that something is amiss, or that a conversational subject has been exhausted. Social and relational conversations also play a different role in low-context cultures. Because time is viewed as an asset, businesspeople like to get right to work, and anything off-topic is considered wasteful.

Low-context communicators may also be uncomfortable with the personal nature of social and relational conversation. In high-context cultures, personal relationships are bound up with business. In low-context cultures, business and personal relationships are usually divided. In low-context cultures the focus is on deriving information from words and their literal meaning.

Good interpersonal relationships may be desirable, but are not deemed essential to the flow of information. This means that documentation is invested with great value. Comprehensiveness in written communication is valued, and specificity and accuracy are seen as an indication of professionalism.

When you're writing to low-context communicators, you'll be expected to maximize the effectiveness of your communication. Make sure you state your point at the beginning, and keep to the subject of the correspondence. Your writing style should make use of simple, consistent sentence phrasing, and use words and terms that have a definite meaning. Avoid poeticism and ambiguity, particularly with business correspondence.

These are the main characteristics of low-context communication:

- it's characterized by directness, precision, and explicit meaning,
- high value is placed on the literal meaning of messages,
- business relationships are task driven and goal oriented,
- verbal reasoning and argument are appreciated, and
- contradiction is rarely personalized.

Cross-cultural communication often involves interaction with people who speak a different primary language than you do. Their understanding of what you're saying might be limited, or you may have to deal with a translator. In these cases, it's important to speak clearly and slow down the pace of your speech. This gives the other person time to translate and process your message.

When speaking or writing, use simple words, thoughts, and phrases. Don't use metaphors, aphorisms, or colloquialisms that don't translate well. You've learned about many of the characteristics of high- and low-context cultures, and how the same sentiment can be expressed differently depending on the context. Now, follow along for examples of high-context messages, followed by low-context equivalents.

High-context: We have some important visitors coming today. It would reflect well on us if they were impressed by the orderliness of our office.

Low-context: Andrew, clean up your desk. It's a total mess and we've got clients coming in today.

High-context: It is somewhat cold today.

Low-context: Will someone shut that window before I get pneumonia?

High-context: We will have to study this proposal further.

Low-context: No. I'm not accepting that proposal.

The differences of high- and low-context style can cause communication breakdown when participants don't understand the true intention inherent in what the other person is saying.

For example, in a low-context culture the meaning of the word "no" is unequivocal. It means something is not accepted. Saying no isn't rude, and is often respected as a sign of directness and honesty. In a high-context culture, saying no directly is avoided. If you call an evening meeting, a low-context person might say "No, I'm busy." A high-context person might say "Yes. An evening meeting is good, though you must be tired from working all day."

An electronics company in a high-context culture is considering switching to a new microchip supplier. A senior manager, Mrs. Tan, sets up a meeting for 11:00 to hear the other managers' opinions on whether or not the company should go ahead with the proposed initiative. After the group exchanges pleasantries, Mrs. Tan broaches the subject of the new supplier. Mr. Lam says that the supplier is respected in the business community. Mr. Yao states he respects Mr. Lam's assessment, even though the supplier is still a very young company.

Fundamentals of Cross Cultural Communication

Mrs. Tan senses that there is a difference of opinion and states that she would be interested in hearing more from Mr. Lam and Mr. Yao. Each manager presents his case in turn. When they're done, the group spends some time in silence considering what they've heard. To conclude the meeting, Mrs. Tan expresses her appreciation to the managers, and relates a story about the importance of respecting friends and family.

The electronics firm's meeting reflected many characteristics of high-context communication:
- the meeting began with time devoted to social matters,
- formal titles were used,
- each manager gave his assessment indirectly by personalizing the new supplier,
- participants acknowledged each other's contribution,
- the group spent time in silent contemplation, and
- the senior manager's decision to maintain the current supplier was implicit in her story about valuing relationships.

A mining company in a low-context culture is considering switching to a new industrial drill supplier. A senior manager, Richard, sets up a meeting for 11:00 with other managers to brainstorm the pros and cons of going ahead with the proposed initiative.

At exactly 11:00, Richard calls the meeting to order, stating "Let's not waste any time" and broaches the subject of the new suppliers. Ellen speaks up first and presents data she's gathered about the cost savings of switching suppliers.

Before Ellen's done Travis interrupts, pointing out a calculation error in her data. The two argue back and forth about whether switching suppliers will be beneficial to the company's profit margin.

When both managers indicate they've made their points, Richard takes back control of the meeting by making a mild joke. He states that if the new supplier can provide the same products at a cheaper price, he's their "new best friend."

The mining company's meeting reflected many characteristics of low-context communication:

- the meeting started with explicit directions about the decision to be discussed,
- the managers related informally to each other, despite differences in rank,
- argument and contradiction were expected and accepted,
- the participants spent little time with social conversation, dealing strictly with the subject of the meeting, and
- the senior manager expressed his intent to base his decision on data.

Case Study: Question 1 of 2
Scenario

You're head of sales for a large multinational pharmaceutical company. Part of your job is to develop business with health services systems in different countries around the world.

Answer each question about communicating in high- and low-context cultures.

Question

Fundamentals of Cross Cultural Communication

You're attending a sales meeting at a large healthcare facility in a high-context culture. The meeting is going well, except for a price concession suggested by one of the senior managers.

Which statements reflect appropriate communication strategies in this situation?

Options:

1. "I'm pleased to meet you, Doctor Gee."
2. "What Senior Manager Lao is proposing has merit, and should be considered with the other options."
3. "Perhaps we should all review the second option that was presented."
4. "Let's get right to work. I know you're all busy."
5. "If no one has anything else to say, let's move on to the next subject."

Answer:

Option 1: This option is correct. Being polite and using titles is a sign of respect in high-context cultures. It's important to show the correct amount of respect and deference to someone based on a person's status relative to your own.

Option 2: This option is correct. It's important to avoid directly contradicting others, even when you disagree. Information that might be disagreeable is presented in a gentle and indirect fashion.

Option 3: This option is correct. High-context communication is indirect. It's important to reflect this style when making requests or communicating decisions.

Option 4: This option is incorrect. In high-context cultures, establishing relationships is an essential part of business. You should take time for introductions and social interactions before business takes place.

Option 5: This option is incorrect. When you're communicating in a high-context culture, silence is acceptable. Participants may need the time to reflect on what's been discussed.

Case Study: Question 2 of 2

You're attending a sales meeting at the head office of a chain of pharmacies in a low-context culture. The meeting is proceeding well, except for when one of the managers challenges your data.

Which statements represent appropriate communication strategies you might use?

Options:

1. "Hi Mike. It's good to meet the new boss. The rest of you – Sheila, Ross, and Jim – I remember from last year."

2. "Let's get right to the point. I'm here to save you at least 10% on your unit cost."

3. "That's not accurate, Jim. You should check your numbers."

4. "Let's have a moment of quiet reflection, so we can all consider the merits of this proposal."

5. "That could be something I would look into at a future date."

Answer:

Option 1: This option is correct. In low-context cultures, social discourse is kept to a minimum in business settings, and casual forms of address are common, even when there's a difference in rank.

Option 2: This option is correct. It's important to be factual and direct. Low-context communicators appreciate it when you come straight to the point.

Option 3: This option is correct. Low-context communicators expect disagreement and debate when a decision is being considered. Contradicting a colleague is rarely personalized.

Option 4: This option is incorrect. Low-context communicators find silence uncomfortable, and may consider this a waste of time.

Option 5: This option is incorrect. Low-context communicators are uncomfortable with ambiguity. They prefer a solid yes or no.

Part of cross-cultural competence involves understanding that you may sometimes unknowingly offend someone. This can happen in both high- and low-context cultures. But you can minimize the risk of a cultural faux-pas by being careful not to use derogatory, or discriminatory language, and by being sensitive to the degree of context required to communicate and understand the true meaning of a message.

SECTION II - EFFECTIVE CROSS-CULTURAL PRESENTATIONS

SECTION II - Effective Cross-cultural Presentations

When you're giving a presentation, it's important to consider the context orientation of the audience members. This will determine the message and style of your presentation. Your message is what you want to communicate – the information you need to convey to your audience. Your style is how you deliver your message – the appropriate method of getting your audience's attention and helping them understand the information you're presenting.

High-context and low-context cultures have very different communication styles. When you are dealing with high-context communicators, you should make use of social and relational conversation to establish your relationship and subtly deliver information about yourself. You should also make sure to use titles to address them, and to adapt your approach to their rank and status. You should avoid directly contradicting them and using casual speech when you converse.

When you're dealing with a low-context communicator, you should avoid too much social conversation, and be direct and to the point. You should feel free to contradict errors and debate points of contention. Friendly, casual speech will be expected, even before you know each other well.

PRESENTATIONS

Presentations

Giving a business presentation can be a nerve-wracking experience. There's a lot to remember. Say this. Demonstrate that. Smile. Look at the audience. Crack a joke to lighten the mood. All the while wondering "Am I connecting with these people? Is my message getting across?" The head of an international software company is giving a speech at the annual general meeting. The audience is made up of senior management and staff from many different countries.

He begins his presentation by explaining that in low-context cultures a presentation usually begins with a joke to relax the audience, whereas in high-context cultures presenters are more likely to begin by apologizing for their inadequacies as a speaker.

"Since this audience includes people from many countries," he states, "I would like to begin by apologizing for not telling a joke." Planning and delivering an effective presentation is always hard work, even when you share a common culture and language with your audience.

But when you're faced with making a cross-cultural presentation, the process becomes significantly more challenging.

When you interact with people from a different culture, more than your words will be different. Your nonverbal communication will also influence your audience's perception, understanding, and ability to make decisions. It's convenient to characterize a culture by its context orientation. However, it's important to consider that within any national culture, there are many subcultures associated with different regions, industries, special interest groups, and even business organizations.

Subcultures often have communication styles that differ from the primary cultural context. If your presentation is based on expectations about cultural stereotypes, it can impede communication rather than facilitate it.

For example, within an industry or business culture, there may be implicit understanding attached to technical jargon. Doctors, architects, computer engineers, and other professions all use jargon to exchange complex information efficiently. Even in a low-context culture, not knowing the meaning of these words, phrases, and gestures defines you as an outsider.

It's important to know your audience's objectives and cultural expectations in order to determine your message and your style of presentation.

Message

Your message is what you want to communicate – the information you need to convey to your audience.

Style

Your style is how you deliver your message. You need to find a culturally appropriate style to get your audience members' attention and help them understand the real meaning of the information you're presenting.

In any type of presentation, it's important to respect your audience. After all, you're speaking only because people have decided it's worth their while to listen to you. This is particularly important in a cross-cultural situation. This will help you avoid cultural mishaps and strengthen your business relationships.

THE MESSAGE

The message

There are many factors to consider before you choose a central message for your cross-cultural presentation. How direct should your message be? Is humor a good way to connect? How is disagreement or bad news expressed? How do you give and receive praise?

The fact is that each situation is different, and there are no rules to help you craft a central message that fits all cultures and all contexts. You'll need to research your audience members and determine what matters most to them.

There are a number of other questions that you need to consider in relation to the culture and context of your audience. You'll need to ask yourself "Who am I?", "Should I present facts or opinions?, "Is the audience interested in short- or long-term benefits?"

Who am I?

Think about how to tell your audience who you are. Should you focus on your achievements or your company's achievements? Does your status matter? If so, how do you relate that status to your audience?

Facts or opinions?

What are your audience members interested in? Are they data-driven and interested in facts and numbers? Or are they emotionally driven, relating to personal stories, anecdotes, and opinions?

Short- or long-term benefits?

What do your audience members hope to get out of your presentation? Are they interested in developing or maintaining a long-term relationship, or are they looking forward to what you can do for them in the immediate future?

Although you may want to impart the same information to different audiences, keep in mind that the focus of your message will be different depending on whether you're doing a business presentation for a high-context or a low-context audience.

In high-and low-context cultures, people derive meaning from the degree of context they require to interpret the meaning of the message.

High-context presentations

In presentations in high-context cultures, people derive meaning from the setting, relationships, and status of the presenter.

Low-context presentations

In presentations in low-context cultures, meaning is derived mainly from the literal meaning of text and speech.

Implicit meaning is important in a presentation to an audience in a high-context culture:

- the presenter relates to the audience emotionally,

- displays of personal engagement and passion are critical to convey the message,
- the status of the presenter is an important part of the message,
- the audience infers a lot of detail from the context of the message, and
- the audience values the emotional content of the presentation,

In a low-context culture, the focus is on the explicitness of the message:
- the presenter relates to the audience objectively
- displays of energy and enthusiasm are critical to convey the message
- the message can often be separated from the messenger
- the audience expects and appreciates supporting documentation, and
- the audience values the clear articulation of data.

HIGH-CONTEXT AND LOW-CONTEXT STYLE

High-context and low-context style

If your message is the "what" of your presentation, your style is the "how." To determine the appropriate style for your presentation, you'll need to examine the different cultural expectations inherent in high- and low-context cultures. Not all cultures prefer the same business presentation style. Audiences in low-context cultures consider long introductions as insincere and a waste of time.

But with a high-context presentation style, it's expected that you'll begin your presentation by recognizing and paying respect to the audience, followed by an acknowledgement of your developing relationship. Your high-context presentation style will be more effective when you keep these and other audience expectations in mind.

High ranking staff run important presentations - Rank and status are important in a high-context culture. The audience will expect high-ranking staff to run important presentations.

Visual aids kept to a minimum - Keep the use of visual aids such as flipcharts or computer slide shows to a minimum. The overuse of these tools may be seen as a sign of disrespect to the intelligence of audience members.

Formal presentation style appreciated - A formal presentation style is appreciated. Spontaneity and improvisation suggest to a high- context audience that a presenter is unprepared.

Several question-and-answer sessions - In a high-context culture, question-and-answer sessions should happen at several planned intervals during the presentation to let the audience consider and digest the information.

Verbal nuance and poeticism valued - The beauty of language also gives context to a presentation. Verbal nuance and poeticism are valued by a high-context audience.

Audience will infer the message - In a high-context culture, the audience will expect to infer the core message from the presentation.

Prolonged eye contact is avoided - In some high-context cultures, prolonged eye contact is disrespectful and should be avoided.

Presenter is deferential to the group - High-context cultures are group-oriented. In a presentation, the presenter is deferential to the audience as a group.

Low-context communicators prefer that you state the core message at the beginning of your presentation, and then prove your point by providing the rationale and data. This linear process seems logical and practical to a low-context audience. But high-context communicators can take offense with this style of presentation.

They may perceive it as an insult to their intelligence that the presenter felt the need to state the obvious to them, rather than letting them infer the message from the presentation. Audience members in low-context cultures have different, and generally more casual, expectations of presentation style.

Any staff member may run a presentation - In low-context cultures, any staff member who is involved in an issue, or who is knowledgeable, may run an important presentation, regardless of rank or status.

Open contradiction of the speaker is normal - The presenter should expect to be debated or openly contradicted in low-context cultures. This is a normal part of the process.

A casual presentation style is appreciated - Although there are formal presentations, in general, low-context audiences enjoy a more casual presentation style.

Question-and-answers sessions are usually at the end - A question-and-answer session is usually held at the end of a presentation, after the presenter has finished presenting.

Humor, spontaneity, and improvisation are valued by the audience - Low-context audiences value a presenter's creativity. This often takes the form of humor, spontaneity, and improvisation.

The core message is communicated early in the presentation - In presentations, audiences expect the core message to be communicated early in the presentation, and then expanded upon.

Eye contact is considered a sign of interest - Both audience members and presenters engage in prolonged eye contact. This is considered a sign of attention and interest.

Presenter may single out audience members - In a low-context presentation, it's not uncommon for the presenter to acknowledge and single out audience members – sometimes for friendly ridicule – regardless of their status.

When you're preparing your presentation, you need to concentrate not on whether a style or technique is right or wrong, but on whether it's appropriate for your audience.

An appropriate presentation uses a style that's adapted to the needs, interests, knowledge, attitudes, and context orientation of the audience.

Keep in mind that the focus of the audience should be on the message and content you're presenting. When you do or say something disturbing or illogical, it shifts the focus to you as a person, and away from the content you're presenting.

Consider this example. John Lee is senior vice president of Mathemetric Consulting Group, an international investment company. His job involves traveling to many different countries, seeking out investment opportunities in emerging and established markets. John is successful in his work because he's aware of the importance of using the appropriate presentation style when he speaks to potential investment partners in other cultures.

John has traveled to a country with a high-context culture to give a presentation to a company. He's just been introduced by the president of the company he's visiting. Follow along as John introduces his presentation to the audience.

Thank you for that kind introduction, President Kam. I am humbled to be speaking today to such an esteemed audience.

Honored guests, I am John Lee, Senior Vice President of Mathemetric Consulting Group.

I am here today to further our relationship with your prestigious company by sharing with you my opinion on investment opportunities in your country.

John's formal introduction was appropriate for a high-context audience.

He began by recognizing and paying respect to the audience, humbling himself in contrast. He also respectfully acknowledged the high rank of the company president. This was followed by an acknowledgement of the developing relationship between the two companies.

Finally, his introduction of the subject of his presentation was ambiguous, indicating that the audience would be able to infer the meaning form the presentation.

It's two weeks later and John has traveled to a country with a low-context culture. He's just been introduced by the owner of the company he's visiting. Follow along as John introduces his presentation to the audience.

John Lee: Wow, thanks for that introduction, Gillian. You were so complimentary I almost didn't recognize myself!

John Lee: Some of you already know me. I see Marta in the front row, and there's Erik too. Erik, I'm glad you could drag yourself away from the coffee machine long enough to come and see me.

John Lee: Well, as Gillian said, I'm John Lee and I work for Mathemetric Consulting Group.

Audience member: Hey, you spelled that wrong!

John Lee: Whoops! I'll fix it later. And no more comments from the kids in the audience. I'll take questions after the show.

John Lee: So, let's not waste any more time. I'm going to show you data about some investment opportunities that are going to make your company a lot of money.

John's friendly casual approach was appropriate for a low-context audience.

He began by acknowledging the company owner, creating empathy by using her first name. He also pointed out individuals in attendance, and made use of a joke to relax the audience. John also used visual aids to enhance his presentation, and he accepted the interruption from an audience member with good humor. Finally, John introduced his message in a factual manner, indicating that his presentation would be data driven.

When you're giving a presentation, it's important to keep in mind that a culture isn't one large homogeneous group.

Subgroups within a culture, or that permeate through many cultures, sometimes develop their own way of speaking, dressing, and relating to colleagues. You'll need to dig deep and find out the high- and low- contexts of the specific group you're presenting to.

One example is the business culture of the information technology (IT) industry. Even within a high- context culture, where business suits are normal for managers, IT professionals may choose the more casual style of dress favored by their industry. An overly formal manner of dress might brand you as an industry outsider.

In any culture, you'll show respect for your audience if you take the time to follow a few simple rules. Follow the dress code of the group to whom you're presenting, make sure you use appropriate visuals, pace your speech, and watch out for double meanings in what you say.

Follow the dress code

Find out the expected dress code and stick to it. Appropriate dress is a way of showing respect for your audience. It's also a way of creating empathy. People are more likely to accept you if you dress as one of the group.

Make sure visuals are appropriate

Make sure that any visuals you plan to use are appropriate to the sensibilities of your audience. Gestures, facial expressions, and the proximity of people to each other have different meanings in different cultures.

Pace your speech

If you're presenting to people who are non-native speakers of your language, don't speak too fast. Pace your speech and give them time to absorb the meaning.

Watch out for double meanings

Watch out for double meanings when you use expressions, metaphors, and anecdotes. These literary devices may not be culturally appropriate or may not translate well. This could cause embarrassment for you or your audience members.

Question

Match each context type to the appropriate characteristics of effective presentation. Each context type may match to more than one characteristic.

Options:

A. High-context
B. Low-context
Targets:
1. High-ranking managers run important presentations
2. Question-and-answer sessions are interspersed throughout the presentation
3. Eloquence and poeticism add to the audience's appreciation of the presentation
4. The core message is presented at the beginning of the presentation, followed by rationale and data
5. There's a reliance on flipcharts and other audiovisual tools to present data
6. Spontaneity and humor are appreciated

Answer:
In high-context cultures, the rank of the presenter indicates the importance of the presentation.

In high-context cultures, questions are answered by the presenter at discreet intervals.

In high-context cultures, the literary quality of the presentation adds to its value.

Low-context communicators expect a presenter to give a core message, and then back it up with proof.

Low-context communicators like visual aids in presentations. In high-context cultures, an over-reliance on these tools may be considered insulting.

In low-context cultures, spontaneity and humor are a sign of cleverness and creativity.

CHAPTER 3 - IMPROVING COMMUNICATION IN CROSS-CULTURAL RELATIONSHIPS

CHAPTER 3 - Improving Communication in Cross-cultural Relationships
   SECTION I - Dealing with Cross-cultural Differences
   SECTION II - Rapport and Cross-cultural Communication
   SECTION III - Overcoming Barriers to Cross-cultural Communication

SECTION I - DEALING WITH CROSS-CULTURAL DIFFERENCES

SECTION I - Dealing with Cross-cultural Differences

Learning how to deal with cultural differences will help you contribute to the creation of an enjoyable work environment, communicate more effectively, and create successful and gratifying relationships.

To deal effectively with cultural differences to improve cross-cultural communication, you need to prepare by becoming aware of your culture, learning about the other culture, and examining any areas of cultural difference. Finally, bridge cultural differences by considering four key areas before taking action: the gravity of the problem; the length and complexity of the relationship; whether your beliefs are based on ideas about one of the cultures being superior; and whether asking for change could denigrate someone's beliefs.

DIFFERENT COMMUNICATION STYLES

Different communication styles

Have you ever been unsure of how to deal with cross-cultural differences in your workplace? Perhaps you've been in a situation like Rosa's. Rosa is the manager of an important two-year project for a global organization. Her team has 15 key engineers, technicians, and administrators from Asian, European, and South American countries, as well as from Canada and the US. Sometimes Rosa feels almost paralyzed with the fear that she'll say something to offend or upset someone.

Rosa knows that when people from different cultural groups work together, misunderstandings can occur. It's easy to fall into an assumption that everyone in a workplace has the same cultural values, but of course that's not true.

People aren't always even aware that their cultural upbringing is influencing them. But when cultural values conflict, people can inadvertently cause offense. But you can learn how to deal effectively with cultural differences to improve your cross-cultural communication. And you can start by understanding cultural impacts.

There are six common ways in which cultures as a whole tend to vary from one another:
- communication styles – language usage and non-verbal communication and their degrees of importance vary between, and even within, given cultures,
- attitudes toward conflict – some cultures welcome conflict with a positive attitude, viewing it as a step toward working out differences, while others try to avoid it,
- approaches to task completion – different ideas of time, relationship-building, and resource access all contribute to varied ideas about how strictly oriented work is to tasks,
- decision-making styles – the roles individuals play in decision-making and the styles they use are influenced by a cultural frame of reference,
- attitudes toward disclosure – some cultures find it inappropriate to show emotions, to explain the reasons for conflicts, or to disclose personal information, and
- approaches to acquiring knowledge – how people learn things varies from culture to culture; some cultures consider cognitive means like counting and measuring more valid, while others value affective learning using symbols and imagery.

Communication styles

Even in the same language, the meaning of "yes" can vary from "maybe, I'll consider it" to "most definitely." And the degree of assertiveness and body language can also add to cultural misunderstandings. For instance, some consider raised voices and exuberant hand gestures to be a sign of conflict, while others consider them to signal exciting conversations.

Attitudes toward conflict

In some cultures, conflict is dealt with directly if it arises, usually by meeting face to face. In other cultures, open conflict is embarrassing or demeaning, and a written exchange may be favored to address the problem quietly.

Approaches to task completion

In certain cultures, people prefer to develop relationships at the beginning of a project, and put the emphasis on task completion later. In other cultures, people focus immediately on the task, and let relationships develop as the work progresses.

Decision-making styles

In some cultures, decisions are often delegated to a subordinate, while in others, the value is on personal decision making. And for group decisions, either majority rule or consensus may be preferred by different cultures.

Attitudes toward disclosure

People in some cultures ask a lot of questions – especially when a conflict arises – that may seem intrusive to those of other backgrounds. Even the sharing of personal information or emotions can cause inadvertent offense.

Approaches to acquiring knowledge

People from some backgrounds may want to research a problem to understand it and identify solutions. Others may want to talk to people with similar challenges to learn what works elsewhere.

Fundamentals of Cross Cultural Communication

Failure to identify differences correctly may lead to labeling other people as "abnormal" or "wrong." An inability to bridge all these cultural differences is the biggest obstacle to effective cross-cultural communication.

Question

What do you think might be the benefits of learning how to bridge cultural differences in the workplace?

Options:

1. Contributing to the creation of an enjoyable work environment
2. Learning to communicate more effectively
3. Helping you create successful and gratifying relationships
4. Helping you get noticed, leading to career advancement
5. Enabling others to adapt to your way of working

Answer:

Option 1: This is a correct option. Bridging cultural differences at work forges understanding and respect, which contributes to an enjoyable work environment.

Option 2: This is a correct option. Overcoming cultural differences can help you communicate more effectively, receiving and transmitting information with better accuracy.

Option 3: This is a correct option. Being able to communicate more effectively and bridge differences helps you create successful and gratifying work and personal relationships.

Option 4: This is an incorrect option. While you might be more productive if you bridge cultural differences, there's no guarantee it will lead to career advancement.

Option 5: This is an incorrect option. Bridging cultural differences isn't about forcing others to adapt to your way of working. It's about finding workable compromises.

PREPARING TO BRIDGE DIFFERENCES

Preparing to bridge differences

Cultural differences in the business community are not as evident as they used to be. Increasingly, there's better understanding and respect for differences, which is an effect of wider global exposure and intercultural literacy. But it's only through individuals learning to bridge differences that this kind of progress happens.

When bridging cultural differences at work, you need to use a structured approach:

- become aware of your own cultural makeup,
- learn about the other culture, whether it's a colleague's, client's, or business partner's customs,
- examine actual or potential areas of cultural differences at work, including communication style preferences, and
- take key considerations into account before deciding what actions to take to bridge cultural differences.

The importance of becoming aware of your culture

Becoming aware of your own cultural makeup will increase your overall cultural awareness. But more importantly, it helps you clarify the values and expectations you hold for yourself and for the people you work with.

To be able to communicate effectively across cultures, you may need to bridge cultural divides by adapting your communication style. If you don't know what that is, you won't be able to bridge differences.

Your cultural makeup prompts some of your ideas and behaviors, ranging from what you think is important at work to the way you communicate. So the first step is to become aware of your culture. Think about the way you talk with other people – friends, family members, and coworkers. Consider the words you use and how you say them, how you ask or answer questions, and how you greet people and say goodbye.

The culture you live in helps determine how you express yourself and how you display pleasure, gratitude, and anger. But cultural conditioning also defines your perception of time and how much privacy and personal space you need. Within each culture, these attitudes help create a smooth approach to life. They're neither right nor wrong – each culture's way is just one among many.

Remember Rosa? Her team is having some cultural clashes, specifically regarding deadlines and the amount of instruction needed to complete tasks. Rosa knows she can't ignore the differences, and begins a structured approach to solving the problem. When examining her own culture, Rosa recognizes that her national heritage contributes to her being task oriented and direct.

Fundamentals of Cross Cultural Communication

Learning about your own culture is only the start. The second step is to learn about other cultures. Everyone should build a cross-cultural literacy about coworkers', partners', and clients' cultures. Understanding cultures different from your own will help you show respect for other people's customs. And learning about other cultures may help you anticipate cultural differences and better understand others' communication.

One way to learn about other people's cultures is to simply talk with them. But you can also do research. Find the countries on a map or in an atlas. Discover what languages are spoken, what forms of government exist, and what religions are practiced. Investigate the histories, and learn who the leaders are.

For example, Rosa's next step to improving her project team's cross-cultural communications is to learn about the members' different cultures.

She observes people on the job, but also gathers information on all the different cultures her team represents. Rosa looks on the Internet and in books, and asks questions. She buys an international holiday calendar and circles all the days relevant to her team. She then researches each holiday and discovers the appropriate way to honor it.

Question

Rosa also thinks about times she's traveled abroad. But she's not sure that will give her valid information, because it's not factual data about other cultures.

Do you think Rosa's previous cross-cultural encounters can give her insight?

Options:
1. Yes

2. No
Answer:
Even personal travel can give Rosa insight into other cultures. For instance, she no doubt met people more or less emotionally expressive than she is, or found herself with either more or less personal space than she'd like.

When you travel, cultural differences can seem colorful, exotic, and appealing. But when you have to work and conduct business, the same cultural differences can lead to disappointed expectations. The laid-back approach to time on an island vacation can cause frustration in an office when deadlines are tight. Alternately, the brisk competence that was so refreshing at a resort may seem overbearing in a coworker.

Once you're aware of your cultural makeup and those of the other parties, you can tackle the third step, which is to highlight and examine any potential or actual areas of cultural differences. Collect as much information as possible about the areas so you know what the situation is.

One way to identify areas of cultural differences is to consider the degree of comfort – or discomfort – you feel in a situation. For instance, consider the matter of personal space, and judge how you feel in different situations.

When you're interacting with people from different cultures, pay attention to when you feel confused, anxious, frustrated, impatient, or angry.

The discomfort you feel can alert you to cultural differences. While it's easier to retreat than face the problem, use your discomfort to help improve your cross-cultural communication.

For instance, think about communication difficulties you may have experienced. Did the pace of conversation seem too fast or too slow to you? Your discomfort can help you compare what you experience to what you expect. Investigate what your discomfort tells you about communicating across cultures and about your own cultural expectations.

Rosa has identified several areas of cultural differences.

Being indecisive

Rosa is from a culture that values directness, so she dislikes when some team members don't give her firm yes or no answers. In her culture, an indirect answer signals indecisiveness; in two of her team members' cultures, it's a sign of deference and respect.

Staring

Rosa is uncomfortable that one of her team members seems to always stare at her. In her culture, staring signals aggressiveness or intimidation. But in the team member's culture, direct eye contact shows attention and esteem.

Standing too close

One of the women Rosa works with stands very close whenever she talks to Rosa. Rosa always finds herself taking a step or two back, and feeling awkward about it. Rosa realizes that her culture expects a large area of personal space, while her coworker's culture is used to a smaller area and less privacy.

Not saying they don't understand

Rosa is particularly frustrated by three team members who never tell her when they don't understand something. In her culture, questions are tools for communication. But in her team members' cultures, questioning superiors signals disrespect.

Always smiling

One of the men Rosa works with is always smiling. Even when Rosa had to talk with him about performance issues, he just smiled at her. Rosa's cultural background perceives such behavior as signaling contempt or disinterest. But in her coworker's culture, a smile radiates sincerity and attention.

Question

You're on assignment to a cross-cultural process management team. Your team is having problems making decisions. You believe cultural differences are the cause, and also think some team members are uncomfortable working with the Sikh employee who wears a turban.

What should you do to prepare to deal effectively with cultural differences so you can improve cross- cultural communications within your team?

Options:

1. Acknowledge that in your culture, people of authority usually make decisions, and few issues are decided by consensus

2. Learn that in some cultures, allowing the person in authority to make decisions signals respect, and that the Sikh employee wears a turban for religious reasons

3. Examine how different decision-making styles can lead to problems agreeing on solutions

4. Learn that one team member thinks that everyone who wears a turban doesn't speak the language

5. Examine different cultures' attitudes toward democracy

Answer:

Option 1: This is a correct option. Becoming aware of your cultural habits, such as how decision- making is usually accomplished, is the first step in dealing with cultural differences.

Option 2: This is a correct option. Learning about the other culture's habits is the second step in dealing with cultural differences.

Option 3: This is a correct option. Examining the areas of cultural difference is the third step in dealing with cultural differences.

Option 4: This is an incorrect option. If one team member has an individual fear or incorrect idea, it's not a cultural habit.

Option 5: This is an incorrect option. Cross-cultural politics isn't the problem within this team – decision making is.

BRIDGING CULTURAL DIFFERENCES

Bridging cultural differences

The first three steps – becoming aware of your culture, learning about the other culture, and examining areas of cultural difference – prepare you for the fourth step, bridging differences. Here, you take appropriate, specific, targeted action to make your cross-cultural communication effective and to respond appropriately to cultural differences. This is the phase when you may modify your non-verbal responses, behaviors, and communication style, or agree on a course of action with the other party.

How you deal with differences will depend on many factors, and no advice will apply to all situations. But bridging cultural differences doesn't mean you give up your own beliefs and behaviors.

In the real world, unless a cross-cultural interaction is complex, long term, and critical to success, you might just need to adjust your communication approach slightly. You might adapt some actions to help others feel comfortable – or the other party may need to adapt – but you aren't necessarily going to follow each step exactly.

A few areas for consideration can help you get things right and decide what type of action is most appropriate:

- Consider the gravity of the differences. Can you easily resolve the difference by modifying your reaction, or does it have a strong impact, creating discomfort, offending you, or negatively effecting business results?
- Consider the relationship you have with the other party. Will you be dealing with the other party long-term or in-depth, or is your encounter going to be brief and in passing?
- Consider whether you believe your cultural habits or the other party's are superior. Do you want to make a change based on these beliefs?
- Ensure change wouldn't offend the other party. Will you be denigrating or offending a person or a group of people if you ask them to change their behavior?

Consider the gravity

Rosa thinks the cultural clashes are causing discomfort and misunderstandings, which in turn are negatively affecting the team's performance. Since the differences are putting the project's success at risk, it's important to do something.

Consider the relationship

Rosa's title is Project Manager, and she's expected to coordinate her team. It's also a long-term project. Her relationship with the team makes it safe and appropriate for her to initiate any actions she finds necessary.

Consider your beliefs about superiority

Rosa has already made the effort to become aware of her cultural make-up and her preferences in terms of working styles. Now she tries not to assume her positions are superior, or to change her behaviors because she thinks another culture's way is superior. In this case, Rosa will involve everyone in determining a solution.

Ensure change wouldn't offend

The clashes in Rosa's team involve misunderstandings about deadlines and performance. Rosa feels confident that she knows what areas she shouldn't touch on, such as asking someone to change their behavior relating to religious beliefs or important cultural values. Rosa has learned enough about her coworkers' cultures to not ask for a change that might offend or denigrate someone on the team.

After thinking about the various considerations, Rosa calls the whole team together to discuss the different cultural expectations regarding timekeeping, deadlines, and the amount of instruction or direction expected. In the meeting, the team creates ground rules for the problem areas. Everyone expresses their views, opinions, and preferences. Rosa also encourages everyone to learn a bit about the team's different cultures to make sure her team becomes aware of its internal diversity.

Rosa explains that the ground rules will create a working environment of respect and known expectations. As a result, uncertainty is reduced and the team's productivity improves.

Rosa could have tried to impose her own views on the multicultural group because "this is the way things are done in my country" or because "I'm the boss." Or she could have ignored all cultural differences in a misguided attempt to show respect. Instead, Rosa avoided ethnocentrism and used the discomfort the cultural differences generated to find a solution that works for everyone.

Question

You're on a cross-cultural team charged with implementing process changes at your company over several years. Your team is having trouble making decisions, and some team members seem nervous around a Sikh employee.

What should you consider before deciding what actions to take to bridge the differences?

Options:

1. Consider how seriously the lack of effective decision-making is hindering the team

2. Consider that your project is complex and long-term, and you all need to work well together for good results

3. Ask yourself if you want change simply because you think your way is the best way

4. Consider that asking someone to change a religious practice would probably offend

5. Consider that the turban is foreign to your culture, and other team members would like the Sikh to only wear it outside of work

6. Consider that consensus decision-making is better, and make yourself promote that style even though it's not part of your culture

Answer:

Option 1: This is a correct option. You need to consider the gravity of a problem and whether or not it has a negative effect before asking anyone to change their behavior.

Option 2: This is a correct option. Consider the relationship between you and your teammates before you take action.

Option 3: This is a correct option. You need to consider your beliefs about superiority before making any decisions.

Option 4: This is a correct option. Ensure that asking for a change wouldn't offend. It's inappropriate to ask someone to change a religious practice.

Option 5: This is an incorrect option. Even if it made other members feel better, asking someone to change a religious habit is likely to offend.

Option 6: This is an incorrect option. Considering the other culture's way superior is biased. Don't make a change based on a belief about superiority.

SECTION II - RAPPORT AND CROSS-CULTURAL COMMUNICATION

SECTION II - Rapport and Cross-cultural Communication

There are many tips and communication strategies you can use to build rapport across cultures. In general, you want to show respect and interest toward a culture, be aware of what the cultural expectations are in relation to business interactions and relationships, and of course, get the other party's name and title right.

Whether a person is from a low-context or a high-context culture, using these guidelines will help you build a strong relationship.

BUILDING RAPPORT

Building rapport

If everyone was alike – with the same culture, language, and customs – you'd always know how to talk and act. If differences were slight, misunderstandings would be minimal. But if everyone was alike, there would be no diversity to spark creativity, open your mind to new ideas, learn new ways to approach the world, or grow a business. But nonetheless, it can be challenging to work with someone who probably speaks a different language, or at least has different habits or expectations.

Many people have similar concerns, because when someone is different in looks, language, or actions, people may initially feel uncomfortable and wonder how to communicate. After all, the influences that make people behave and interrelate the way they do are complex, and outsiders may feel intimidated or confused. But there are many benefits to being able to have good cross-cultural communications.

Being able to recognize and understand differences in culture will allow you to communicate respect and interest toward other cultures, communicate effectively, and build successful working relationships with coworkers and clients. Whether you're a salesperson, an executive, or a member of a customer service team, it's important to create positive and gratifying cross-cultural communications. And the way to do that is to build rapport.

The word "rapport" means a relationship marked by harmony, accord, or affinity. Such a relationship doesn't happen immediately, and must be built carefully. In the global business community, you need to know how to build rapport with people from other countries and cultural contexts.

Language alone can cause difficulties. Consider the fact that, presently, there are 5,000 to 6,000 different languages spoken worldwide. The English language is the third most common language in the world – Mandarin Chinese and Hindi are numbers one and two. But even when countries share the same language, there are still many other cultural differences.

It's difficult to give country-specific advice on building rapport. Not only can cultures change, but individuals often show characteristics that differ from those considered typical of their national cultures. But there are some general tips and strategies that can be used in most cross-cultural situations, and that will help you build rapport across cultures. Many cultures have a variant of the ethical standard called the Golden Rule – "treat others as you would like to be treated."

But in multinational business dealings, the way to build rapport might be to follow a Global Rule – "treat others as they would like to be treated."

Question

Lauren and John work together on a virtual team. They're from cultures widely separated by language, customs, and religion. Lauren would like to know more about John's home and background.

Do you think Lauren will offend John if she acknowledges their cultural differences by asking questions?

Options:

1. Yes
2. No

Answer:

Lauren might be afraid that by acknowledging John as different, she'll offend him. But if she avoids asking any questions about their cultural differences, she'll never be able to get the information she needs to build rapport with him.

When building rapport, you need to show respect and interest toward the other party's culture, and be aware of the person's cultural expectations regarding business interactions and relationships. This, of course, includes getting the other party's name and title right.

SHOWING RESPECT AND INTEREST

Showing respect and interest
In cross-cultural encounters, asking people about their cultures allows you to better understand cultural tendencies and expectations. Such courtesy and respect encourages a reciprocal reaction, building rapport and making it easier to communicate. In addition, gathering information about the culture helps you meet the other people's needs more effectively, and helps ensure you minimize disappointments from missed expectations.

When you show respect and interest toward people, whether they're clients, coworkers, or business partners, you let them know you're interested in their countries and you respect the mutual cultural differences.

This provides you with a chance to start off on a positive note. Many people are greatly appreciative when someone from another country shows an interest in – and some knowledge of – their culture. In addition, learning about the other party's culture will give you an idea if there are any cultural protocols you may need to be aware of.

Asking openly about someone's culture should be done with respect and without ridiculing any habit or belief that may sound unusual. There are also other actions to take in order to show respect and interest:
- learning new words in someone else's language will no doubt impress, and possibly put a smile on the person's face,
- using the country's media – listening to music, reading books, and watching movies about and from the country – will let you be engaged with the culture,
- relating positive travel stories – such as food from the country or region you have tried and liked, people you've met, or other experiences you had – can allow you to converse on matters of common interest, and
- following international news will help you figure out what the politics are like, what the current popular stories are, and what might be of vital interest to the other person.

Question

Rico, whose company is based in South America, is going to meet with Fiona, who represents a new business partner in Great Britain.

What strategies can Rico use to build rapport by communicating respect and interest toward Fiona's culture?

Options:

1. Say a few words in English when he greets Fiona
2. Talk about a book by an English writer he read recently
3. Give an opinion about a recent political scandal

4. Tell Fiona about the food poisoning he got in London

Answer:

Option 1: This is a correct option. Learning a few words in Fiona's language will demonstrate Rico's willingness to work to build rapport.

Option 2: This is a correct option. If Rico immerses himself in Fiona's culture, it will help him communicate better and give them something to talk about.

Option 3: This is an incorrect option. While keeping up to date on the political situation is good, you don't want to cause offense. Instead of giving his opinion, Rico could try asking Fiona for hers.

Option 4: This is an incorrect option. Relating travel experiences that reflect poorly on someone's country won't build rapport.

BEING AWARE OF CULTURAL EXPECTATIONS

Being aware of cultural expectations

Differences in cultural expectations can have a major impact when people from dissimilar cultures discuss business. Awareness of cultural protocols enables you to understand them, so you'll be less likely to be offended – or to cause offense with your behavior. For example, the handshake is used as a greeting in many different cultures throughout the world. However, handshakes can be of varying lengths and firmness. If you aren't aware of these cultural differences, you can inadvertently transmit misleading information.

That's why it's so important to be aware of what the other party's cultural expectations are in your business interactions and relationships. In every culture, members focus on what their society deems important. You need to know not just language and phrasing expectations, but how important context is to a society.

With regard to communication, context refers to how much people rely on things other than words to convey

meaning. Anthropologist Edward Hall was the first to describe cultures as "high context" and "low context" according to inherent differences between societies. These types of cultures typically forge different types of relationships:
- high-context societies forge close and deep connections over a long period of time, and
- low-context societies have many connections, but they're of shorter duration or were formed for a specific reason.

In general, cultures that favor low-context communication will pay more attention to the literal meanings of words than to the context – the body language, relationship bonds, and other unspoken expectations – that surrounds them. But every culture, and every business situation, will have high and low aspects. For instance, families are high-context regardless of the surrounding culture; members of a family know how to behave and often communicate indirectly without spelling out information in words.

Whether a culture is high- or low-context will influence how readily you're accepted.

High-context

In high-context societies, most of the information being transmitted and received isn't in the spoken or written part of the message. Much is either in the physical context or in the relationships of the people involved. Trying to enter such a culture – even briefly, such as for a business negotiation – is difficult, because you can't instantly create close relationships and you don't have the same internal context information.

In high-context cultures, accepted behaviors are not made explicit. Most members know what to do and what to think from years of interaction with each other. For instance, families are usually a high-context environment, and new family members can find it difficult to feel like they fit in.

Low-context

In low-context societies, most information is vested in written or spoken words. These societies encourage the formation of many relationships, and the environment contains much of the information needed to participate. As a result, they are relatively easy for an outsider to enter.

In low-context cultures, cultural behavior and beliefs can be spelled out explicitly, so you know how to behave. The important thing is to accomplish a task rather than feeling your way into a deep relationship. For example, a short-term task force is usually a low-context environment.

To communicate effectively across cultures, especially during business dealings, which group the other party belongs to will affect your approach. For a high-context culture, to build rapport, you should focus first on building trust. Creating relationships will generally be the longest part of the process when dealing with members of high-context cultures. However, once you're accepted as an insider, you'll have strong relationships with a high degree of loyalty.

High-context cultures value trust. To build a relationship, there are several things you can do:

Fundamentals of Cross Cultural Communication

- Keep your promises, and don't tell someone from a high-context culture that you'll do something unless you know you can deliver.
- Be dependable, honest, and genuine, and don't try to be someone you're not. Most people can sense falseness.
- Project a reputable image, and promote your company's solid reputation. Make sure the other party knows that your company has a good track record.

Question

Which are appropriate actions you could take to build rapport with high-context cultures?

Options:

1. Make sure the other party knows your company has been successful in business for many years
2. If you say you'll e-mail a report by the end of the week, make sure you follow through and do it
3. Begin right away on the task at hand, and let your trustworthiness develop with the relationship
4. Make sure you have an interpreter to help with language difficulties

Answer:

Option 1: This is a correct option. Projecting a solid reputation is a good idea when dealing with a high-context culture that values relationships.

Option 2: This is a correct option. Being dependable and keeping promises is a good strategy when interacting with high-context cultures.

Option 3: This is an incorrect option. High-context cultures need a base for the relationship first, before committing to working together.

Option 4: This is an incorrect option. Differing cultural expectations can exist even when people speak the same language, and an interpreter won't help with that aspect.

Low-context cultures tend to value logic, facts, and directness. When building rapport with low-context cultures, get right to the point and try to avoid euphemisms. People from low-context cultures may not understand hidden meanings. In low-context cultures, relationships matter, but the task or work is more important. People from these cultures generally want to spend less time getting to know someone and more time getting details and specifics.

Relationship building is still important in low-context cultures, but you build rapport in slightly different ways:

- Ask questions. You have to know the explicit details to communicate effectively with low-context cultures.
- Provide details. Give relevant information about products or services, providing facts and figures to back up what you say. Low-context cultures value proof.
- Be succinct. Get to the point quickly, since low-context cultures value economy of words.

Taku comes from Japan. He's meeting with Werner, whose company is based in Germany. Taku wants to build rapport with Werner, so he treats Werner the way he would like to be treated. Taku keeps his promises to send Werner the information he wants. Taku focuses on his company's reputation, as well as his own, to project a dependable and caring demeanor. But Taku can't understand why Werner seems impatient with him, and the meeting doesn't go well.

Question

What could Taku have done to have an easier time building rapport with Werner?

Options:

1. Give Werner succinct details about the subject at hand
2. Keep the conversation to the point
3. Tell Werner that Taku's company is solid and reliable
4. Go into more detail about all the connections the two companies have in common

Answer:

Option 1: This is a correct option. Being succinct but providing lots of details is a good choice when dealing with a low-context culture like Werner's.

Option 2: This is a correct option. Keeping a conversation on track is a good tactic when dealing with a low-context culture like Werner's.

Option 3: This is an incorrect option. Projecting a dependable image is especially important when dealing with a high-context culture, but Werner is from a low-context society.

Option 4: This is an incorrect option. Emphasizing the degree of connectedness is good when dealing with a high-context culture, but Werner is from a low-context society.

GETTING NAMES AND TITLES RIGHT

Getting names and titles right

The other important component of building rapport across cultures is to be sure you get names and titles right. While, of course, you need to pronounce the names correctly, you also have to consider the level of formality expected. In some cultures, it's not appropriate to address people by their first names. As a general rule, it's a good idea to address everyone by their titles and surnames until – or if – they ask you to call them by their first names.

Many people have names that are difficult for people from other cultures to pronounce or spell. If you encounter such a name, have the person write the name down, and then make notes about phonetic pronunciation.

Reviewing prior communication from the person you're trying to build rapport with can help. It will indicate whether someone prefers to be referred to by a first name or surname. You can often determine the preferred approach from the tone of the communication.

For example, titles are widely used in high-context cultures, and these cultures tend to be more aware of status and rank than low-context cultures.

Aiko is Asian, and she's about to present an advertising proposal to Zack Brown, who's a doctor from Australia. Follow along with their conversation as Aiko tries to build rapport.

Aiko: Hi Dr. Brown, I'm so pleased to see you!

Zack: Hi there, and please call me Zack. So this is your first visit to Australia?

Aiko: Yes, it is. Well Zack, I know you're a busy person and I don't want to waste your time. Shall we get started on the proposal?

Zack: If you like.

Zack sounds a little unhappy.

Question

In the previous scenario, what did Aiko do correctly while trying to build rapport with Zack?

Options:

1. She showed respect and interest toward Zack's culture
2. She demonstrated awareness of Zack's cultural expectations regarding business interactions and relationships
3. She got Zack's names and titles right

Answer:

Option 1: This is an incorrect option. Aiko had an opening to show her respect and interest in Zack's culture, but she said nothing about Australia.

Option 2: This is a correct option. Aiko was aware that Australia is a low-context culture, and got right to the point of the meeting.

Option 3: This is a correct option. Aiko began the conversation more formally, calling Zack "Dr. Brown," but appropriately responded to Zack's low-context informality.

SECTION III - OVERCOMING BARRIERS TO CROSS-CULTURAL COMMUNICATION

SECTION III - Overcoming Barriers to Cross-cultural Communication

Everyone at some point in time will recognize behaviors in themselves that can hinder cross-cultural communication.

The communication barriers of ethnocentrism, stereotyping, and misunderstanding can be overcome with watchful diligence, an open mind, and techniques to reduce verbal and nonverbal misinterpretations. By taking action to overcome these barriers, you can enhance your communication with people from other cultures.

COMMUNICATION BARRIERS

Communication barriers

Society today is made up of many cultures, languages, and customs, yet often people don't know how to talk or act in the presence of a person from another culture. And in a global business environment, it's imperative to be able to understand people who come from countries and cultures different from your own.

Working in cross-cultural environments can be challenging, but it's also interesting and rewarding. But good communication is vital, because when communication is difficult, relationships may be difficult too.

If you ignore communication differences, it inevitably leads to miscommunication. This can then trigger conflicts that can cause people to feel unwelcome or offended.

By being tolerant of differences – and using techniques for cross-cultural communication – you can overcome any cultural obstacles. When you're in cross-cultural

situations, you may encounter some barriers to communication:
- ethnocentrism occurs when people believe in the superiority of their own cultural group, and dislike or misunderstand all other groups,
- stereotyping happens when people have a standardized mental picture that represents an oversimplified opinion, prejudiced attitude, or uncritical judgment about a group of people, and
- misunderstandings or misinterpretations occur when there's a failure to fully grasp what's meant, and can lead to disagreements or discord.

ETHNOCENTRISM

Ethnocentrism

The first barrier, ethnocentrism, hinders cross-cultural communication because people who are ethnocentric evaluate others cultures only according to the norms, standards, practices, and expectations of their own cultures. It's a temptation that's hard to resist, because it's natural to think your accustomed way is the right way to do things. After all, experiences with different cultures can generate intense positive or negative feelings that range from delight and excitement to confusion, fear, and even dislike.

That's why monitoring your emotional reactions to people or customs from other cultures can give you insight into values that may reflect an ethnocentric perspective.

You may encounter negative feelings, which can unveil beliefs in the inherent superiority of your own culture and the inferiority of the other culture. Or you may have positive ethnocentrism, which elevates your perception of the other culture because your own seems inferior or somehow lacking.

Either form of ethnocentrism interferes with truly understanding and communicating with people from another culture.

It's natural to have some ideas that spring from an ethnocentric perspective. But after you identify those thoughts, you can take action to overcome the ethnocentrism:

- Suspend judgment of the other culture. Be aware of value judgments, because they block understanding.
- Ask yourself what you would do if you were in the other person's shoes. Try to consider problems and experiences from the other person's point of view, remembering that you don't have to agree with, like, or prefer the one that isn't yours.
- Think about what you've learned from other cultures in the past. Be open to learning from other cultures. Be curious. Learn all you can about the culture, probing into statements, viewpoints, and behaviors.
- Most people behave rationally. Assume that the behaviors you think are strange have a rationale you don't yet understand.

Question

Which types of barriers to communication do you think the following phrase typifies?

"The French know the best way to do things."

Options:

1. Ethnocentrism
2. Stereotyping
3. Misunderstanding

Answer:

Option 1: This is a correct option. This statement says the French culture is better than the speaker's culture, which is ethnocentric. Ethnocentrism can be positive, as in this case, but it still interferes with true understanding.

Option 2: This is a correct option. Stereotyping may come from an ethnocentric view of a particular culture, but it results in an oversimplified and generalized attitude about all French people.

Option 3: This is an incorrect option. Misunderstanding – or not grasping the meaning of something – isn't typified in this ethnocentric, stereotypical statement.

STEREOTYPING

Stereotyping
The second barrier, stereotyping, often arises from ethnocentric perceptions of superiority and inferiority. Stereotypes distill ethnocentric ideas into broad generalizations. Stereotypes leave no room for individual differences or exceptions. Any new information is channeled into the existing category and only strengthens the category and confirms the existing viewpoint. And when people hold preconceived ideas about a culture, they're resistant to ideas or individuals that challenge the stereotype.

When people don't interact with other cultures frequently, stereotyping due to overgeneralization is especially common. The human mind naturally seeks order and patterns, especially in new situations, so the mind creates rules or generalizations.

In addition, when people feel threatened, the human mind can presume negative motives or draw negative inferences from generalizations. This forms the basis of prejudice. To cross this cultural barrier, you need to be aware that everyone holds stereotypes of others, and that experiences may lead the brain to reinforce these stereotypes.

To overcome stereotypes, make sure you're aware of any generalized ideas or images you hold of other social groups or people from other cultures. Avoid expressions that associate particular behaviors with specific races, nationalities, or ethnic groups, and challenge generalizations you encounter.

Question

If you catch yourself thinking "The French always think they know best," what do you think you could do to overcome this barrier to communication?

Options:

1. Be aware you're thinking that all French people act superior
2. Think of all the French people you know, and how varied they are
3. Catch yourself when thinking about the French being superior, and redirect your thoughts
4. Think about all your experiences with French people, and categorize them by how superior they act
5. Think about all the times you've felt like your own culture has the best way of doing things

Answer:

Option 1: This option is correct. Being aware of how you stereotype people or cultures is the first step to overcoming this communication barrier.

Option 2: This option is correct. This is an oversimplified, prejudiced attitude about French people, and you should challenge the stereotype.

Option 3: This option is correct. The statement stereotypes all French people, and you should stop yourself from making generalizations like that.

Option 4: This option is incorrect. Categorizing your experiences in this manner will only reinforce any stereotype you may have.

Option 5: This option is incorrect. Identifying your ethnocentrism about your own culture won't help you overcome a stereotype about another culture.

MISUNDERSTANDINGS

Misunderstandings

The third barrier is misunderstanding. Consider the example of Jan, a process consultant from the Netherlands. Jan went to India to help a company install a new performance management system. The people he worked with seemed to disagree with almost everything he said. They kept shaking their heads from side to side. Jan became flustered by what he perceived as constant rejection of what he was saying.

What Jan didn't know was that in that region of India, a side-to-side head shake is a sign of agreement and encouragement, not of "no," the way it would be in the Netherlands. Jan was falsely attributing a negative response to the action, which led to a misunderstanding. And this simple misunderstanding of a local custom resulted in Jan having a difficult time performing his job.

Many misunderstandings stem from false assumptions that attribute incorrect motivations to others' behavior. But you can overcome misunderstandings, whether they're caused by differences in language, in etiquette expectations, or in non-verbal behaviors. Educating yourself about other cultures will help you understand the meanings of gestures, expressions, and body language.

And using clear, simple language – avoiding slang and local expressions that may not translate, for instance – will help reduce spoken misunderstandings. Be sure to always ask for clarification and explanation, and speak slowly. Remember that both sides have to encode and decode each message effectively to ensure understanding.

Educate yourself about other cultures

To educate yourself about another culture, make sure you learn the cultures' gift-giving customs, as well, of course, as your own company's policies and any legal restrictions on gifts. When scheduling your communication and interactions, learn about and respect holidays and time-zone differences. And when entertaining, learn about food and alcohol customs. For example, Muslim people don't drink alcohol or eat pork, and Hindus don't eat beef.

Use clear, simple language

When you speak with someone with a limited knowledge of your language, stick to strict rules of grammar. Use complete sentences. Eliminate slang or jargon that is peculiar to a particular group. Sports metaphors should be used carefully, if at all. Use short, simple sentences, and use more nouns than pronouns. Be exact in your word usage, and choose words that are easily understood, such as "effective" rather than "efficacious."

An American software company service manager is preparing to discuss a problem a Greek customer is having. Select "Before" and "After" for an example of how communication can be improved in this situation.

Before

The manager thinks he'll say, "In reviewing your call history I can see that we have sent a technician to look at this problem several times. I am sorry the service call is taking more than one occurrence to resolve your problem. Don't worry; we'll make this A-OK." He wants to make a gesture of encouragement, and thinks the sign for "OK" – touching his index finger to his thumb and making a circle – will make his customer feel hopeful about a resolution.

After

Upon reflection, the manager revises the statement to be more straightforward, and says "I see that a technician has looked at this problem several times. I am sorry the problem has taken more than one service call to fix." He educates himself about the cultural meanings of gestures, and discovers that the gesture that means "OK" in his country can be considered obscene in Greek, Brazilian, and Turkish cultures. Instead of making the gesture, he smiles.

Of course, while history and culture shape customs and rituals, there's always variation within any groups. No matter how much groups differ from each other, within each group there will be shy people and bold people, honest and dishonest, aggressive and submissive types. While there are patterns within each group that are more alike than they are different, it's important to remember that any culture is made up of many types of people.

Question 1 of 2

Fundamentals of Cross Cultural Communication

Match the examples of cross-cultural communication to the type of barrier they reflect. One example will not be used.

Options:

A. Maria believes the way things are done in her country is the only right way to do things

B. Nigel thinks all people from island nations are bad at time keeping

C. Ruth uses local expressions when talking to Barbara, and Barbara has a hard time following the conversation

D. Raul thinks he doesn't need to learn Spanish, even though his company started doing business in Mexico

Targets:

1. Ethnocentrism
2. Stereotyping
3. Misunderstanding

Answer:

Thinking that your way is the only way is an example of ethnocentrism, which is a belief in the inherent superiority of one culture over another.

This is an example of stereotyping, which is the generalization that all people from one culture act in the same way.

This is an example of misunderstanding. Misunderstandings can easily happen if someone uses slang or colloquial expressions that may not translate well for someone from another culture.

Question 2 of 2

Match the common barriers to cross-cultural communication with actions that can be taken to overcome them.

Options:

A. Ethnocentrism
B. Stereotyping
C. Misunderstanding

Targets:

1. Lisa doesn't jump to conclusions about an unusual habit her new coworker from China has

2. Omar realizes his parents always said that people from a certain country were lazy

3. When Jorge joins a cross-cultural virtual team, he learns about all other cultures, and gets a global clock and calendar

Answer:

Suspending judgment about cultural habits that may seem strange to you is a way to overcome the barrier of ethnocentrism, or believing that your way is the only right way.

Becoming aware of any generalization you may make when dealing with someone from a different country is one way to overcome the communication barrier of stereotyping.

Educating yourself about other cultures is a good way to overcome the barrier of misunderstandings in communication.

GLOSSARY

Glossary

A

authority - The power or right to give orders and instructions and to make decisions.

B

barrier - An obstacle that stands in the way of effective communication.

body language - Non-verbal communication consisting of posture, gestures, body position, facial expressions, and eye contact. Often culturally specific in meaning.

business etiquette - Formal and informal etiquette and rules of order applying to interactions with coworkers, work colleagues, and business partners within a business, industry, or economy. See etiquette.

C

collectivism - A Hofstede cultural dimension that points to a culture in which ties between people are strong, the group is more important than the individual, conformity is expected and rewarded, and communication relies on shared knowledge and assumptions as well as intuition, social status, and nonverbal cues. See also individualism.

collectivist - A person who identifies with a group, such as a family or team, and prioritizes the group's needs over the needs of any individual.

colloquialism - An informal word, term, expression, or pronunciation specific to a geographic region.

context - The social circumstances or environments that determine, refine, or change the implicit meaning of a communicated message.

coworker - A person working with another worker, usually at or near a similar level of authority or responsibility in the workplace hierarchy.

cross-cultural communication - Communication where the degree of cultural difference between the communicators is distinct enough to create dissimilar interpretations of the meaning of exchanged messages.

cultural behavior - Behavior that is typical of the majority of people within a particular culture.

culture - A set of shared attitudes, values, beliefs, customs, and practices that characterizes an organization or group.

E

eloquence - The expression of emotional content in a formal communication method using persuasive and inspiring language.

ethnocentrism - A belief in the superiority of one's own cultural group and a dislike or misunderstanding of other groups. Ethnocentrism is a barrier to cross-cultural communication. See barrier.

etiquette - A set of written and unwritten rules of conduct that govern social interactions within a culture, social class, or group.

expectations - Culturally based anticipations and predictions about how people will communicate.

F

false assumption - A conclusion that is not based in fact, or is based on incomplete knowledge of the facts. Prejudice and bias influence false assumptions, which are a barrier to cross-cultural communication. See barrier.

faux pas - An unintentional violation of accepted social norms, such as customs or etiquette.

feedback - Information communicated to an individual, work unit, or team about job-related performance or behavior.

feminine culture - A culture in which gender roles are fluid, men and women assume nurturing and assertive roles, there is equality between the sexes, and quality of life, people, and the environment are valued. See also masculine culture.

H

Hall, Edward T. and Mildred R. - Anthropologists who developed categories of cultural behavior, which they theorized drives cross-cultural communication.

high-context communication - Communication where meaning is derived from the physical, social, and geographical contexts in which the message is sent and received. See also low-context communication.

high-context culture - A culture where high-context communication predominates. See high-context communication.

Hofstede, Geert - A Dutch social scientist who studied the impact of culture on behavior, and identified five national, cultural dimensions. See also Hofstede's Model of Cultural Dimensions.

Hofstede's Model of Cultural Dimensions - A study of 116,000 IBM employees in over 40 countries around the world that led to the identification of four national, cultural dimensions: power distance, uncertainty avoidance, individualism, and masculinity. The dimension long-term orientation was added later. See power distance, individualism, masculinity, uncertainty avoidance, and long-term orientation.

I

indirect communicator - A person who communicates indirectly using inference, suggestion, and implication to inform the meaning of a message. Indirect communicators are more common in high-context cultures. See high-context culture.

Individualism - A Hofstede cultural dimension that points to a culture in which ties between people are loose, personal achievement and individual rights are important, and people communicate primarily through words. See also collectivism.

Individualist - A person who identifies with self, and who prioritizes individual needs over the needs of the group.

initiative - An organizational program, project, or effort that has a specific purpose, goals, and objectives. See project. J

J

jargon - The technical vocabulary of a particular profession or special interest group.

L

long-term orientation - A Hofstede cultural dimension that distinguishes among cultures based on how people think about the past, present, and future.

low-context communication - Communication where there is little or no implied meaning other than that contained in the literal message of the words. See also high-context communication.

low-context culture - A culture where low-context communication predominates. See low-context communication. M

M

masculine culture - A culture in which gender roles are clearly defined, men are dominant and women are nurturing, money and possessions are important, and work matters. See also feminine culture.

masculinity - A Hofstede cultural dimension that assesses a culture based on gender role divisions. See also masculine culture.

N

netiquette - Etiquette for using computer networks and the internet. See etiquette.

nonverbal communication - Unspoken or unvoiced elements of communication used to send messages, modify meaning, and convey emotion. See also body language.

P

personal behavior - Behaviors peculiar to an individual. While people may be influenced by culture, their own personal preferences mean that their behavior may not mirror their culture fully.

polite fiction - A situation where participants are aware of a truth, but pretend to believe in an alternative version of events to avoid conflict or embarrassment.

power distance - A Hofstede cultural dimension that assesses the degree to which the less powerful members of a culture, institution, or organization accept the unequal distribution of power.

project - A collaborative enterprise with a defined beginning and end that is planned to achieve particular goals and objectives.

R

rank - A person's position within a defined hierarchy.

rapport - Harmonious accord between two people.

resistance - Noncompliant behavior; a force that tends to oppose or retard an action or a change.

S

slang - Informal words and expressions particular to a language, culture, or social group. See also jargon.

status - A person's social or cultural value or standing relative to that of others.

stereotype - A representation of a person or a group based on formulaic, distorted, or generalized characteristics that are perceived to be typical of a group or culture.

stereotyping - Applying stereotyped mental images, ideas, or impressions to an identifiable person or group. Also, a barrier to cross- cultural communication. See barrier.

T

thought pattern - A logical progression of reasoning.

U

uncertainty avoidance - A Hofstede cultural dimension that assesses a culture's tolerance for uncertainty, risk, ambiguity, and unstructured situations.

universal behavior - Behavior that applies to everyone, regardless of their culture.

universalist - A person who applies the same rules to all, without making exceptions for family, friends, or members of their in-group. Universalists view situations objectively.

REFERENCES

References
1. **Doing Business Internationally, Second Edition: The Guide to Cross-Cultural Success** - 2003, Walker, Danielle and Thomas Walker, McGraw-Hill
2. **Working on Common Cross-cultural Communication Challenges** - http://www.pbs.org/ampu/crosscult.html
3. **Communicating Across Cultures** - http://www.culture-at-work.com/highlow.html
4. **Bridging the Culture Gap: A Practical Guide to International Business Communication** - 2004, Penny Carte and Chris Fox, Kogan Page
5. **Managing Cultural Diversity in Technical Professions** - 2003, Lionel Laroche, Butterworth-Heinemann
6. **Communicating Across Cultures** - 2000, Don W. Prince and Michael H. Hoppe, Center for Creative Leadership

7. **When Cultures Collide: Leading Across Cultures Third Edition** - 2006, Richard D. Lewis, Nicholas Brealey Publishing
8. **Communication in the Workplace** - 2007, Baden Eunson, John Wiley & Sons.
9. **Cross-Cultural Communication: The Essential Guide to International Business, Revised Second Edition** - 2003, Bannon, Gerard, Kogan Page
10. **Cultural Intelligence: Living and Working Globally, Second Edition** - 2009, Thomas, David C. and Kerr Inkson, Berrett-Koehler Publishers

www.ingramcontent.com/pod-product-compliance
Lightning Source LLC
Chambersburg PA
CBHW020917180526
45163CB00007B/2769